This Book Will
Make You Fearless

Jo Usmar

First published in Great Britain in 2016 by

Quercus Editions Ltd
Carmelite House
50 Victoria Embankment
London EC4Y 0DZ

A Hachette UK company

ISBN 978 1 78648 140 5
Ebook ISBN 978 1 78648 139 9

10 9 8 7 6 5 4 3 2 1

Editorial and design by Bookworx

Printed and bound in Great Britain by Clays Ltd, St Ives Plc

Contents

Introduction

Don't be scared! Everything's going to be fine. The text from your friend arrives just as you're about to walk into the job interview that you've been dreading for weeks. 'Easy for you to say', you mutter, as you put your phone away with shaking hands. Your heart is thumping so hard in your chest you're sure everyone in the vicinity can hear it. You reach for the door handle and realise your palms are sweating. 'I can't do this', you think, 'I'm sweaty and disgusting. I don't know what I'm doing. They'll see right through me. I'll make a total fool of myself. It'll be just like last time. It's better if I don't go in at all.' Breathing hard, you turn away, having made up your mind to leave. Head home. Give up. But the door swings open. 'Ready?' the smiling woman asks. You stare at her, frozen, not knowing what to say.

Fear. It's the ice crawling up your spine signalling that danger is close. It's the whoosh of horror screaming at you to RUN AWAY. It's the insidious angst influencing every decision you consider. It's the heart-thumping, leg-shaking, hard-to-breathe reality of facing new things, both 'good' and 'bad'. But guess what? Everyone feels scared sometimes. Yep, even that huge guy who bellows his political views at the top of his voice to anyone who'll listen in the pub. He's terrified about his upcoming custody battle and the fact that he knows, deep down, that the views he constantly espouses are probably rubbish.

Fear takes many forms and affects everyone differently. It can hold us back, get us stuck in a rut and make us judge ourselves and others. It can be very painful, paralysing us both emotionally and physically. It can make us terrified of moving forward, so we hang on to things we know aren't working in our lives and that fail to make us happy. It can make us feel powerless and depressed. It can alter the course of our entire lives and make us question ourselves and others – until we can't see any way to change things. If fear was a person, they would be the most unpopular dinner guest in the history of socialising. But – and here's the big BUT – that's unfair. There are some good things about fear. No, seriously, hear me out.

You won't ever be able to get rid of fear completely – and nor should you want to. We, as humans, are designed to experience the full range of emotions available in the mood shop, and fear is one of them. It's our inbuilt threat-detecting device, flagging up danger, hazards and peril. It's nature's way of trying to protect us – and we need that. Sometimes. Just, not all the time. (Especially not when we're on a date or negotiating a pay rise.) So yes, fear has its place, and this book will teach you how to accept that feeling frightened is an essential part of being human and then how to push through it. For without fear, we might never experience the rush of pride, pleasure and confidence that comes from doing something that tests us, that shoves us out of our comfort zone, that makes us think, 'YES, I did it!'

Without fear we'd never get to be brave.

And that's the kicker: you can't ban fear, delete it or extinguish it, but you can work with it to achieve great things. Fear doesn't have to hold you back or dictate your life. Being fearless means acknowledging your fear, saying 'yes, I see you' and then making the choice to take action anyway. And the good news is you've already taken the first step by simply picking up this book.

Why choose this book?

This Book Will Make You Fearless is a concise and practical guide to recognising your fears, battling through them and getting what you want out of life. Based on a cognitive behavioural therapy framework, there are tips, tools and examples throughout that offer simple and effective ways of dealing with fear in all its many guises. You'll learn to recognise how fear affects you personally – how it influences your mood, body, thoughts and behaviour. This will enable you to notice negative patterns, so you can stop yourself charging down well-worn, destructive paths. Understanding fear's differences from, and relationship to, anxiety and worry is an essential part of the book and will enable you to better understand why you respond the way you do to certain situations – so you can alter these reactions next time. You'll learn to accept that change isn't bad, that 'settling' can be a recipe for disaster and, most importantly, that you do have choices. This book will teach you to start seeing fear differently – not as a big STOP sign blocking your ambitions, but as a confirmation that you're heading in the right direction because you're testing yourself and growing. All of which will force you to accept (perhaps grudgingly) that the world isn't tilted against you and that you're not a victim of circumstance. You *choose* how you deal with whatever happens to you. This knowledge will make you feel brave, confident and independent enough to make decisions that are right for you. It will make you stop thinking you are less than you are. Cut yourself some slack!

How to get the most out of this book

This is a manual for overcoming fear. As such, you'll have to dedicate time and energy into making some changes. You wouldn't just read a book on captaining a steamer ship and then leap aboard, deck shoes akimbo, expecting to sail the seven seas. You'd do research, you'd make notes and you'd practise. Practise. Practise. Practise. Yep, that sounds boring and a lot like hard work, but you're altering belief systems that have been buried deep within you for years, if not your entire life. The only way to break those beliefs down and reassess them is to get busy and take action. There are some strategies that will deliver immediate results, but for long-term change prepare to practise, take things seriously and give it your best shot.

+ Read the chapters in numerical order as each builds on the last. You'll be able to dip in and out when you've got the hang of things, but you don't want to miss something you may later rely on

+ Please try all of the strategies (identified by Ⓢ). Don't skip past them or skim-read them, thinking, 'That's not for me' or 'I don't need that'. This stuff really does work. By disregarding it you may skip something that could help you, but by trying all the strategies, you're giving yourself the best possible chance at beating your fears

+ Buy a notebook that you only use for working with this book. Yes, a real-life notebook with actual pages you can write on with a pen. As antiquated as it sounds, writing things down has been proven to aid memory, increase concentration and make things seem more 'official' in your head. Also, you'll be able to flip back and see how far you've come as you progress

+ Practise. We've already covered this bit, but I've added it in again because it's so important

Just by picking up this book you've made the conscious decision to take control of your fear and stop it controlling you. You've already taken the first step in feeling braver and that deserves some recognition. Give yourself a pat on the back, pour yourself a stiff gin or do a little jig. You should be proud of yourself for not settling for a life half-lived. Remember: you can make changes and you can cope with whatever life throws at you – no matter how frightening it seems.

I

The
Frighteners

What are you scared of? What is it that holds you back, keeps you up at night and makes you feel frustrated, anxious or insecure? This chapter will teach you the first steps in feeling fearless: identifying your fears and recognising how they affect your life.

What is fear?

Fear is a primitive human emotion. It's our inbuilt alarm system, flagging up danger and triggering the physical 'fight or flight' response (see Chapter 3) – so we can either fight the threat or run from it, screaming at the top of our lungs.

On a very basic level, fear can be categorised into two types:

Conditioned fear: A fear that is 'learned', usually by something 'harmless' being repeatedly associated with something scary, such as visiting the dentist reminding one of experiencing pain and discomfort. These connections can come from your own memories, stories you've heard, novels you've read, television programmes you've watched or even news reports – pretty much anything that sticks in your mind and makes an impression on you.

Unconditioned fear: A fear that is wholly instinctual; an evolutionary survival mechanism. For example, the fear you feel when standing on the edge of a crumbly cliff or when facing a furious rhinoceros.

The difference between fear, panic, anxiety, stress and worry

Many people use these words interchangeably, and, in everyday use, that's fine. However, if you want to better understand the nitty-gritty of what's going on in your head and in your life, it's crucial to recognise the subtle differences between them. This book deals with fear, anxiety and worry as they are defined here:

Fear An emotional response to a known and well-defined threat that can be identified (even if it's imaginary), i.e. 'I am scared of X and Y'.

Panic The most extreme form of fear. Panic is triggered by something your body construes as life-threatening that is happening to you in the present moment – right *now*.

Anxiety Anxiety is an emotional response, usually anticipatory in nature, to an unknown or ill-defined threat or perception of danger, i.e. 'I feel anxious about the possible outcome of X or Y'.

Stress A feeling (both emotional and physical) of being under pressure, i.e. 'I feel stressed about this deadline, but I know I'll make it' versus 'I feel anxious about the possible repercussions of missing my deadline'.

Worry The thought processes that trigger anxiety and fear, i.e. 'What if...?'

Feeling afraid at certain moments is totally and utterly normal. Fear keeps us safe, stopping us from strolling across a motorway, setting fire to our hair or walking down dark, dingy alleys alone at night. It's also a natural reaction to doing something new, to being put under pressure or to deliberately freaking yourself out. If you are faced with something frightening, but trust you aren't in actual danger, your physical response can actually be quite enjoyable. It's what people mean when they say they're 'buzzing' and why they take part in extreme sports, go on rollercoasters or watch horror films. If you're about to go on stage the 'rush' of adrenaline can push you to succeed and do your very best.

However, sometimes fear can get carried away with itself and materialise too regularly, or over things that don't warrant it. Fear is a sly beast and can sneak its way into all areas of our lives, making everything seem harder and less achievable. Where once you were confident and happy, you suddenly find yourself sipping a drink you didn't order because you're nervous about offending the bar staff; feeling angry about everything and griping at people, but not knowing why; staying in a relationship or job that makes you miserable, but feeling unable to leave. Fear, anxiety and worries can warp your sense of reality until you see opportunities as problems and problems as insurmountable. The ability to push through your fear becomes impossible. What might be a minor bump in the road for someone else becomes an impassable crater for you.

Gratuitous fear can be incredibly debilitating because you don't know it's out of context or in any way misleading – you trust it totally. If your body is screaming, 'RUN FOR THE HILLS!' it's pretty hard to ignore it. And so when thoughts like, 'I can't do that' or 'It'll be a total disaster' pass through your head, you accept them as facts, hiding away, making excuses and avoiding dealing with stuff. This, in turn, makes you feel guilty, resentful, angry, insecure or frustrated. Not feeling able to take chances or make changes chips away at your self-esteem, making you feel even less able to face the next situation, issue or problem. It's a vicious circle.

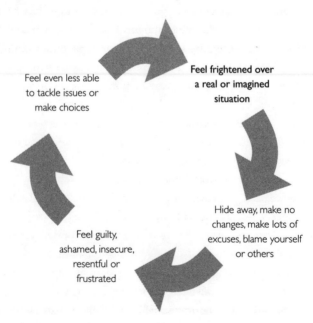

Feel even less able to tackle issues or make choices

Feel frightened over a real or imagined situation

Hide away, make no changes, make lots of excuses, blame yourself or others

Feel guilty, ashamed, insecure, resentful or frustrated

Are you suffering from an anxiety disorder?

If you feel anxious all the time and believe you may be suffering from an anxiety disorder (such as phobias, obsessive compulsive disorder (OCD), paranoia, social anxiety, panic disorder, generalised anxiety disorder or post-traumatic stress disorder) please visit your doctor for further help. However, don't dismiss this book – the strategies will help you too.

Whether you're scared of one big thing or lots of little things and whether your fear is characterised by occasional jitters or a generalised dread, the fact that you picked up this book is a great step forward in seizing back control from your fear gremlins. Retreating from difficult situations, avoiding changes and settling for unsatisfactory or unhappy situations isn't any way to live. While fear is a natural part of life, it doesn't have to – and absolutely won't if you follow the strategies in this book – rule your life.

What are you scared of?

If I asked you that question, right now, what would your answer be? Perhaps something along the lines of:

+ Giving a presentation at work tomorrow
+ Telling my flatmate I'm moving out
+ Having sex for the first time with my new partner
+ Taking my driving test
+ Trying to find a new job
+ Breaking up with my boyfriend
+ Telling my brother I've broken his laptop
+ Asking my friend if I can borrow some money from them
+ Looking fat at my sister's wedding
+ Asking for a pay rise

Great! Well, it's obviously not great that you're scared of those things – no one's going to crack open the bubbly at the thought of breaking up with someone, even if the dumpee is a chump. But recognising your fears and being honest about them is a positive first step. Seeing common worries listed like that should reassure you that becoming frightened is completely natural. Everyone feels scared sometimes. It's part of life. It's how we know we're pushing ourselves out of our comfort zone. It's our body's way of saying either, 'Wow, this could be exciting', or 'WARNING: IT'S THE END OF DAYS'.

The problems start when anxiety and worries over these things become crippling and stop us taking action. When the thought of making changes, standing up for yourself, asking for favours, looking towards the future or facing up to potentially uncomfortable truths paralyses you with fear. When you don't dump the chump or ask for that totally deserved pay rise because fear has inhibited your ambitions, making you feel trapped, powerless and paralysed. So, while 'having to get a new job' would naturally cause a few worries for anybody, if you feel that you can't even contemplate it without breaking into hives, that entering the job market is akin to leaping feet-first into a pool of piranhas, then something's not right. Your fear-o-meter is out of whack.

Completing the next strategy is the first step in finding out why.

⑤ Your fear list

Make a list of everything you're fearful about right now. Don't overthink it or get in too deep (we'll get to that later – something to look forward to!). Just anything that springs to mind, for example:

What I'm scared of:
✦ Moving house
✦ Making new friends

- Going to Jonny's party on Friday night
- Having to make small-talk at my in-laws' on Saturday
- The suspicion that my partner might be an alcoholic
- My dad's deteriorating health
- Getting old
- Being attacked by a stranger
- Someone I love dying
- The threat of terrorism

Forcing yourself to break down your fears like this will make fear itself seem less all-encompassing. Stopping to assess things in a systematic way is an important step in making fear lose its aura of ubiquity.

Congratulations: you have just scratched the tip of the fear iceberg.

Meet the fear iceberg

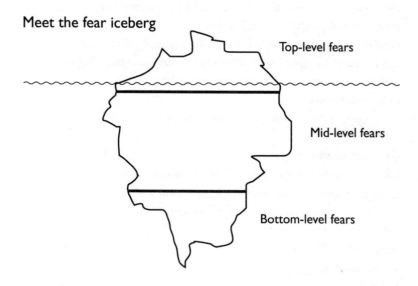

Top-level fears

All the things you wrote down in the fear list strategy are your top-level fears. External events and things happening out in the world that you can point to and go, 'You. You're a real pain in my ass.'

These kind of fears can be split into two groups: those that you can't do anything about and those that you do have some control over.

Fears you CAN'T do anything about	Fears you CAN do something about
Ageing	Making new friends
Death	Finding a new job
War/famine/ecological disasters	Signing up to a dating app
A family member becoming ill	Splitting up with your partner
Becoming ill yourself	Having kids
Being attacked by a stranger	Moving house
Having an accident	Losing or gaining weight
What other people are thinking	Giving up drinking

You probably recognise many of these fears and could add a few more of your own. That's not because you're scared of everything; you're not a paranoiac or bag of nerves.

The reason lots of us fear many things is because top-level fears are created by mid-level ones and, while top-level fears are situation-driven, mid-level ones are emotionally driven. They're about your state of mind. As such they spread like wildfire, making one fear lead to two, three, four, five hundred. So, what are these hideous fear fire-starters?

Mid-level fears

+ Rejection
+ Humiliation
+ Disapproval

+ Vulnerability
+ Change
+ Failure
+ Success
+ Responsibility
+ Helplessness and powerlessness

Now we're talking. If you're scared of disapproval, of people judging you, it follows that you'll be scared of meeting new people, insecure about how you look and fearful of attending events. Just as if you're scared of being vulnerable you'll be wary of intimacy, of starting new relationships, of making new friends and of losing the ones you have. These are the emotions driving your everyday situation-based top-level fears.

Working out your mid-level fears

Ⓢ Your mid-level fear list

Have a look at your original fear list from page 14. Taking them one at a time, think about what mid-level fear may be behind it. What emotion are you running from?

Top-level fear	Mid-level fear
I've found a lump under my armpit	Vulnerability and helplessness
My partner's bad temper	Vulnerability and rejection
Applying for a loan	Rejection and disapproval
Public speaking	Humiliation
Job interview	Failure or success
Starting internet dating	Rejection, disapproval and vulnerability

If, instead of saying, 'I'm scared of public speaking', you said, 'I'm scared of being humiliated', you'd be cutting much closer to the bone and getting to the heart of your fear. You'd also be able to recognise the breeding ground for many of your other fears. If, rather than saying, 'I'm scared of this job interview', you said, 'I'm scared of failing, of not being good enough, but also of succeeding – of the pressure that might bring', you'd be giving a much more honest account of what's actually going on.

Which brings us on to the deepest, murkiest level of the fear iceberg: your bottom-level fear. Drum roll please…

Bottom-level fears

The thing driving all of your fears, the thought behind your most tempestuous sleepless nights, the reason your fingernails are bitten to bloody stumps, the fertiliser for the sludgy muck from which grow the weeds of your discontent, is…

'I can't cope'

ARGH! THE HORROR. THE TERROR. THE UNMITIGATED HIDEOUSNESS. No, seriously, that's it. That's the golem feeding your terror: the thought that you can't cope. That when push comes to shove, you won't cut it, you won't handle it and will eventually be found curled up in the foetal position weeping and hugging a bottle of gin. That's what we're all really scared of.

So, at the top level it's:
'I can't cope with getting older'
'I can't cope with being single'
'I can't cope with changing my life plan'
'I can't cope with making new friends'
'I can't cope with asking for a pay rise'

And why don't you think you can cope with them? Because...

'I can't cope with rejection'

'I can't cope with humiliation'

'I can't cope with change'

'I can't cope with more responsibility'

'I can't cope with failing'

'I can't cope with feeling vulnerable'

'I can't cope with feeling helpless'

'I can't cope with disapproval'

Yes, that one tiny thought 'I can't cope' is the root of all your trouble. And the reason it's so powerful is because you don't even recognise it as just a thought any more – it's become a belief. A belief is an acceptance that something is real and true with or without any evidence. And this particular belief is so established, so bedded into your psyche, that you don't even notice when it rears its ugly head and starts messing with your business. You just accept it and feel like crap. You accept a thought like, 'I can't handle failure' as a fact, without challenging it or analysing it, and then skip your job interview, cancel your date or shelve your dream for running your own business. In a nutshell: you overestimate the danger and underestimate your ability to cope.

The symptoms of fear

⑤ Your symptom check list

Please tick all of the symptoms you recognise in these boxes. Going through this list will get you thinking about your personal response to fear and will help you to categorise those reactions – your emotions, physicality, behaviour and thoughts – and understand how they are all connected. Something we go into in much more detail in Chapter 2.

Thoughts

- ❏ 'I can't cope'
- ❏ 'What if' worries about the future
- ❏ Worst-case scenarios (often stemming from 'what ifs')
- ❏ Black-and-white thinking (it's either right or wrong, with no grey area)
- ❏ Mind-reading ('They're thinking I'm not good enough')
- ❏ Catastrophising ('This is a disaster, everything is ruined')
- ❏ Ruminations on the past
- ❏ Laying blame on yourself ('This is all my fault')
- ❏ Excuse thoughts ('I'll do it when I've lost some weight/ moved house')
- ❏ Taking things personally ('This always happens to me')
- ❏ Laying blame on others/not taking responsibility
- ❏ Comparing yourself to others unfavourably and unfairly
- ❏ Becoming self-absorbed
- ❏ Self-absorbed thoughts (making everything about you)

Physicality

- ❏ Racing heart
- ❏ Increased respiratory rate
- ❏ Muscle aches and pains
- ❏ Chest pains/'tight' chest
- ❏ Tension in neck and shoulders
- ❏ Pins and needles
- ❏ Numbness in extremities
- ❏ Difficulty swallowing
- ❏ Difficulty sleeping
- ❏ Exhaustion
- ❏ Increased or decreased appetite
- ❏ Increased sweating
- ❏ Low libido
- ❏ Nervous tics
- ❏ Nauseous

Behaviour

- ❑ Settling for something that isn't what you'd hoped for
- ❑ Avoiding the subject or issue completely
- ❑ Snapping at people or acting irritably
- ❑ Becoming a workaholic or withdrawing from work
- ❑ Isolating yourself socially or being overly sociable, i.e. saying yes to events you don't want to attend just to be 'doing something'
- ❑ Being aggressive or confrontational
- ❑ Over- or under-eating
- ❑ Increased drinking/smoking/drug-taking
- ❑ Nail-biting/skin-picking
- ❑ Being distracted, finding it hard to concentrate
- ❑ Reduced personal hygiene/not looking after yourself
- ❑ Narrow focus on one thing (work, appearance, social life)
- ❑ Difficulty making decisions
- ❑ Reckless attitude
- ❑ Constantly seeking reassurance
- ❑ Always seeking to please
- ❑ Constantly saying 'sorry'
- ❑ Procrastination and/or avoidance

Moods/emotions

- ❑ Fearful
- ❑ Anxious
- ❑ Panicky
- ❑ Guilty
- ❑ Ashamed
- ❑ Insecure
- ❑ Frustrated
- ❑ Angry
- ❑ Defensive
- ❑ Sensitive
- ❑ Overwhelmed
- ❑ Depressed

Why do you feel this way?

How much you fear and what you fear is totally unique to you. You may have one overarching fear that takes up all your headspace, you may be bogged down by many little fears that have cumulated into a general feeling of angst, or you may occasionally experience a hit of terror when it's least convenient. Whatever you're scared of, though, there are things that will have influenced how you dealt with these feelings in the past and how you continue to deal with them now.

Your nature

You were born with certain traits. How those traits shift and change as you grow and experience life is totally dependent on what happens to you and how you manage it, but essentially there are bits of you that are here to stay. And one of those bits may be a susceptibility to fear, anxiety, stress and worry. If you are of a sensitive nature your fight or flight reflex will be triggered more quickly and more regularly than other people's and your body will take longer to calm down.

Your upbringing

Our impressions about ourselves, others and the world are formed in childhood. Kids generally accept what they are told and what they are shown to be 'truths' by their parents and teachers because they have no basis for comparison. Their ideas surrounding self-worth, judgement, acceptability, achievement and normality are established very early on and these ideas turn into staunchly held beliefs as they grow up. If one of your parents was a worrier and constantly said, 'Be careful', 'Are you sure you can do that?', 'Maybe you're not ready for that yet' or 'WOAH! Get off that bike immediately', the impression that everyday things are dangerous or threatening will have taken root in your mind. And, more importantly, the impression that you can't cope with those things will have taken root too.

Of course, parents want their children to be safe but when they say, 'Be careful' what they're actually saying is, 'I'm scared you'll get hurt and I can't cope with you getting hurt'. However, what you hear as a kid is, 'I don't think you can cope with getting hurt'. This has a huge influence on children. If you constantly hear, 'I don't think you can cope with that' from your parents, you will inevitably start questioning your ability to cope. Why wouldn't you?

Also, the environment you were brought up in will have played a part in how you view 'success' and 'normality'. If you had a very fractured childhood, perhaps moving around a lot with a succession of carers or parental figures, this may have instigated a fear of intimacy and stability, or conversely, a staunch desire for intimacy or stability, leading to either a fear of being without a relationship, job or home, or a fear of being with one! Mid-level fears will be of rejection, disapproval, vulnerability and responsibility.

Similarly, if you grew up in a very traditional household (whatever your culture), this will have shaped your view of acceptability, of what makes someone 'a success' both professionally and personally. For example, if your parents believed that it's a man's job to earn a living, while a woman's place is in the home, this will have affected your plans for the future and your fear of their disapproval.

Culture

Pop culture, national culture and religious culture all affect what is considered to be successful, desirable and acceptable. Every culture has its own expectations surrounding behaviour – even counter-cultures do. The boundaries you push, the chances you take and the choices you make will all be dictated and influenced by where and how you live.

Life events

What happens to you throughout your life plays a huge part in how you measure your ability to cope and consequently whether you feel fearful or otherwise. Experiencing trauma at any age can either reinforce existing core beliefs you have about yourself or it can shatter them.

External and internal demands

+ External demands: those put upon you by family, work, friends, laws, rules and government, etc. In short, any pressure or expectations put upon you, rather than those you put upon yourself
+ Internal demands: what you expect of yourself according to your own personal definitions of success and acceptability

The demands put upon you by both others and yourself ramp up your stress levels, which can, in turn, ramp up your anxiety and fear levels. If you feel overwhelmed by what's in front of you, you can start to fear it – you can fear the act of completing the task, the repercussions of completing it, or even just the process of thinking about completing it.

Next steps...

In this book you will find strategies that will enable you to recognise your fears, put them into perspective and then choose how to act. The worst thing about fear is that it makes you feel you don't have any choice. You can feel helpless about the patterns that are repeating in your life. The techniques detailed in these pages will show you that your perceived lack of choice is total rubbish – you do have choices. Lots of them. You have the power to influence and make changes. And you ARE brave enough to make them.

Thoughts to take away

✓ Feeling fearful about things is totally and utterly normal.
  Fear is a natural part of life and accepting this fact will make
  you feel more confident about facing whatever it is that
  frightens you

✓ Understanding how your emotion-driven (mid-level)
  fears feed your situation-driven (top-level) fears will make
  whatever you're scared of lose its aura of invincibility

✓ You can't get rid of fear totally, but you can learn to push
  through it. Fear springs from the belief that you can't
  cope, but the strategies in this book will convince you
  that you can

2

CBT Versus Fear

This chapter explains what cognitive behavioural therapy (CBT) is, how it works and introduces you to strategies that will teach you how to face your fear and push through it.

What is CBT?

The trouble with the world of therapy is that so much of it sounds pretty terrifying. Rather than conjuring up images of you sitting with your feet up, sipping a glass of Chablis and feeling at peace with the world, the words 'cognitive behavioural therapy' can summon images of white coats, tin-foil hats and padded rooms. Which isn't ideal when dealing with issues surrounding fear. BUT – another big BUT – don't let the name deceive you. CBT isn't scary in the slightest. It's a leading treatment for a range of issues, including anxiety, insomnia, depression, low self-esteem and, yep, fear. Pioneered by Dr Aaron T. Beck in the 1960s and recommended by the National Institute for Health and Care Excellence (NICE), CBT is a problem-focused treatment that teaches you practical strategies for dealing with the tricky issues in your life.

The fundamental basis of CBT is 'it's not what happens to you that affects you, it's how you *interpret* what happens'.

Example: Lucy is leaving

Lucy picks up the phone to call her parents. She has to tell them she's moving to another country for work. She accepted the new job two months ago, but keeps finding excuses not to tell them: 'Dad's feeling ill, it would be cruel to tell him now', 'Mum just witnessed that terrible car crash – she'll be too worked up to hear my news'. Now Lucy's moving date is only four weeks away and her parents still don't know. The guilt and worry have been eating away at her and she can't stop imagining their despair and disappointment. But knowing that she can't avoid it forever, she dials their number, heart thumping in her chest. Her dad answers: 'Lucy! How nice to hear from you. Wait a sec, your mum wants to tell you all about this lovely card she received from the neighbour.' As she listens to her mum's story, she bites her nails. 'I can't tell her now,' she thinks. 'She's so happy, it'll ruin her day.' When her mum asks her how she is, Lucy replies, 'Fine, Mum. Just checking in. Got to go. Bye!' and puts down the phone with shaking hands – having still not told them.

Lucy's interpretation of accepting the job abroad is: 'My parents won't be able to cope with me leaving and I won't be able to cope with hurting them'. These are her top-, mid- and bottom-level fears, showing unease surrounding change, responsibility, disapproval, rejection and vulnerability. As well as genuine concerns regarding their feelings about it, she has projected many of her own fears about this big change in her life upon her parents. These thoughts have influenced her behaviour (she puts off telling them), which affects her mood (making her feel guilty as well as fearful), which in turn affects her body (racing heart, sweaty palms, nervous twitches and breathlessness).

And that's what CBT is all about: seeing the connections between your thoughts, emotions, body and behaviour. I've illustrated this in a nifty diagram called a mind map using Lucy's situation as an example (see page 30).

Lucy's behaviour not only aggravates the fears she already has, but it creates new anxieties and worries. Because she's avoided telling her parents for so long, thoughts like, 'What if my mum cries? Oh God, what if my dad cries? What if they don't speak to me again? What if I've ruined everything?' clog up her head, making her feel worse physically and emotionally and further weakening her resolve to tell them.

If Lucy had been aware of these patterns she would have been able to see this domino effect at work, recognising that her thoughts, body,

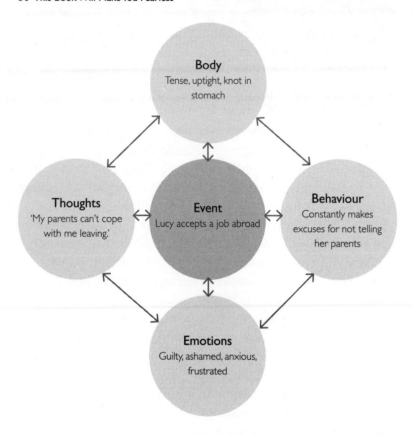

behaviour and mood were conspiring to make her feel frightened. Knowing this, she could have sought out different interpretations of the event – more positive and, most importantly, more *realistic* interpretations. Because that's the catch. When you fall into these vicious cycles, you lose any sense of perspective. You believe your fears to be unassailable facts. In Lucy's case, this 'fact' is: 'My parents can't cope with me leaving'. However, it's not a fact, it's just a thought and THOUGHTS AREN'T FACTS.

Write these three words down in your notebook, in your diary, on your fridge and on the back of your hand – wherever it's going to hit you between the eyes every day. This is your new motto for life, your new mantra, your new rallying cry whenever fearful thoughts bash on the door of your mind. THOUGHTS AREN'T FACTS. They're just propositions put forward by your biased brain. They represent how you feel about your ability to cope at that one particular moment in time, which is unlikely to be a fair representation, given that you're scared to death in that moment. These thoughts often have no basis in reality, but you believe them because they're your thoughts, so they must have some weight, right? NO. Your brain is doing some weird stuff at the moment and it can't be trusted. You need to become aware of this so that the next time thoughts like, 'I can't do this' or 'I can't cope with that' fly through your head like malevolent crows, you can catch them and get them to stop squawking.

Ⓢ Your own 'thoughts as facts' mind map

Draw the mind map on page 32 in your notebook.

1 Think of the last negative thought that passed through your head dressed up as a fact. Perhaps it was something like, 'I can't do this', 'He hates me' or 'They think I'm crap at my job' – anything negative about yourself that you stated as a fact rather than just as a thought. Put it in the middle 'thoughts' circle.
2 Fill in the rest of the mind map by considering how this one thought affected your body (did your heart start racing or your shoulders slump?), your behaviour (what did it make you do or think about doing?) and your emotions.

This is a hugely important strategy, showing how your thoughts, emotions, body and behaviour are all connected. You may think the little

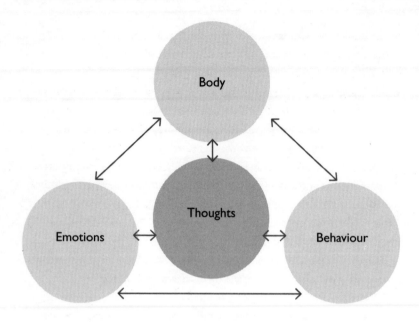

thought 'I can't cope with my new job' doesn't do any harm. But you'd be terribly wrong. That one thought is like a wrecking ball, smashing apart your self-esteem. Thoughts like that matter. They have a ricochet effect on what happens next – on how you choose to deal with (or not deal with) whatever it is you're facing. You need to start cross-examining these thoughts.

⑤ Cross-examining your so-called 'factual thoughts'
Look for evidence to disprove the thought you based your mind map on. To force your sceptical mind to do this, ask yourself:

+ Have I ever attempted something similar before? If so, how did it go? Can I learn anything from how that played out to help me now?

+ Have I got any abilities or skills that may come in useful?
+ Am I being unfair on myself and/or other people?
+ What is the alternative interpretation?
+ Is this alternative interpretation more realistic than my original thought?

Try to be fair on yourself. Just now, when you're feeling terrified, it's highly unlikely you're being fair about your ability to cope, right? Accepting that simple truth will make you feel more able to consider that there might be alternative views to the doom-and-gloom ones your mind is offering up.

Lucy's alternative interpretation

After Lucy gets off the phone to her parents, having avoided telling them her news for the fifteenth time, she opens her notebook and sees 'THOUGHTS AREN'T FACTS' scrawled in large black marker pen on the front page. She also sees the mind map she drew out, showing how her thoughts, body, behaviour and emotions are both influencing, and being influenced by, each other. She sits down and thinks, 'Okay, I'll give it a shot – why might telling them not be the catastrophe I imagine it to be?' Grudgingly (because she genuinely believes it will be a catastrophe and this exercise is a waste of time), she jots down these notes:

Have I ever attempted anything similar before?
+ I told them I was going to Australia for my gap year before and the conversation went well
+ They coped fine with my living abroad then and I'm not going to be so far away this time
+ I remember that telling them in their own house over a glass of wine helped as they felt relaxed and calm, so perhaps I should go to theirs rather than tell them over the phone

Do I have any skills or abilities that could help?

+ I'm calm under pressure so once I get going I should be able to talk them through my decision to leave

Am I being unfair on myself and/or other people?

+ Both. I'm being unfair on myself because I am strong enough to cope with leaving them – and I'll come back all the time! Plus, if I don't like it I can always come home for good. And I'm being unfair on them because while yes they'll be sad I'm moving away, they'll also be really proud of me for doing so well in my career and they'll know it's a great opportunity for me. Plus they'll really love coming to visit

What are the alternative interpretations?

+ That both I and my parents will be able to cope with my leaving. I'll come home often and they can come to visit

Is this alternative interpretation more realistic than my original thought?

+ Yes. I think that while they may be a bit sad I'm going, they'll ultimately be happy for me

What a massive difference this makes to Lucy's mood. She has to admit that these points aren't ludicrous or nonsensical. In fact, they're actually far more realistic, considered and rational than the totally vague 'They won't cope with me leaving' fear that was dictating her actions before. This not only lifts her mood, but calms her body down and makes her reconsider her behaviour. Maybe she can tell them, because even if they do break down and the meeting with them goes terribly, she's now got a list of persuasive points as to why her moving won't be so bad. She can tell them those and try to make them feel better – just as she's made herself feel better. Her new mind map looks like this (see opposite):

Body
Increased heart rate,
but in control

Thoughts
'My parents will be sad
that I'm leaving, but will
understand my decision
and be happy for me.'

Event
Lucy accepts a job abroad

Behaviour
Explains her decision to
her parents at their house
over a glass of wine

Emotions
Calm, resolute, excited

Your behaviour, body and thoughts are all intervention points – change one and it'll change the others for the better. Lucy focused on changing her thoughts about the event, which then lifted her mood, relaxed her body and gave her the confidence to tell her parents (behaviour).

However, the first thing she could have done is calm down her body. If she felt her fear very physically, with a racing heart and sweaty palms, she would have found it impossible to think of potential positive points. Calming down her body would have calmed down her mind, so she could then have re-assessed her thoughts, which would have influenced her behaviour and her mood.

How you react to things is incredibly personal and in this book you'll learn how to recognise your own patterns so you can interrupt them, giving you back control over your thoughts, body, mood and behaviour.

How to understand fear using CBT

Psychologist Arnold Allan Lazarus believes there are two separate stages to our interpretation of a stressful situation:

Primary appraisal: Is there a problem?
Secondary appraisal: Can I cope with the problem?

In Lucy's example, her primary and secondary appraisals were: 'Telling my parents is a problem and, no, I can't cope with it'. Your state of mind will decide your primary appraisal. If you are feeling positive and confident you are more likely to view issues as things to be overcome rather than stumbling blocks to be feared, i.e. 'Yes, there's a problem, but I can cope with it' or 'No, it's not a problem, more a challenge'.

Imagine you've applied for a job and are waiting to hear whether you've got an interview. You wait… and wait… but hear nothing. You assume that you haven't been successful and contact the HR representative at the company to ask for some feedback so you can see where you fell short: 'Oh, but we'll be seeing you tomorrow, won't we?' the woman you speak to asks. 'At your interview? Didn't you receive our email?' Your heart rate picks up and you start breathing faster. 'Tomorrow?' you squeak. 'Yes! See you at 10am,' she chirps.

Positive primary appraisal: 'Wow! I got through. Thank God I called or I would have missed the interview. This is not a problem, just a great opportunity.'

Fearful primary appraisal: 'This is definitely a problem. I'll never be ready by tomorrow. What a nightmare!'

If you decide that it is a problem, you'll move on to your secondary appraisal – can I cope with it? – and your decision will depend on your mid-level fears.

How frightened you feel – or whether you feel frightened at all – will be influenced by how in control you feel, how long the situation's been going on for, how many internal and external demands are on you at the time, the deadlines you have to meet and your levels of self-esteem and self-belief.

Positive secondary appraisal: 'It's a bit of a nightmare, but I can spend the whole of tonight preparing and I'll cope with it.'
Fearful secondary appraisal: 'I don't have time to get ready tonight so I'll be humiliated tomorrow. I can't cope with this!'

A fearful secondary appraisal will cause your blood pressure to skyrocket, your mood to plummet and you'll be likely to act in unhelpful ways (such as behaving defensively and aggressively in the interview). Whereas, if you'd already decided it wasn't a problem (or it was a problem but you could cope with it), you'd feel calm physically, your mood would be nervous but upbeat, and you'd be more likely to behave in ways that would encourage a good result.

I have illustrated a negative primary and secondary appraisal of this situation in the mind map overleaf.

CBT will teach you to recognise when you're making automatic negative appraisals and when you're stating thoughts as facts – so you can challenge both. Practising the strategies included in this book will soon ensure that your primary and secondary appraisals are automatically more

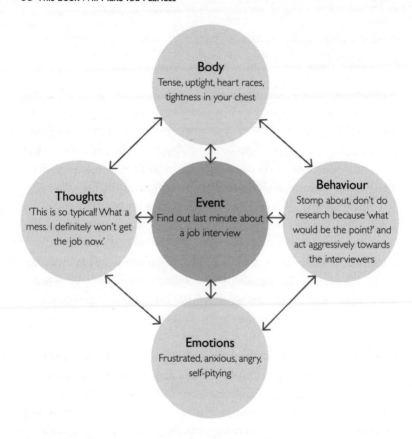

Body
Tense, uptight, heart races, tightness in your chest

Thoughts
'This is so typical! What a mess. I definitely won't get the job now.'

Event
Find out last minute about a job interview

Behaviour
Stomp about, don't do research because 'what would be the point?' and act aggressively towards the interviewers

Emotions
Frustrated, anxious, angry, self-pitying

positive than negative. You'll actively try to find solutions to problems, see opportunities rather than obstacles and will feel generally more in control of your choices.

Why are your appraisals negative?

Our lives are busy. Incredibly busy. Even if you're sitting on the sofa reading this in your pants, I bet your mind's racing and you feel as if there are a thousand things you should be doing instead. Technology has developed at such an extraordinary rate we're bombarded with information 24/7. It's perhaps no surprise that our attention spans are getting shorter when we have apps, tweets, status updates, likes and comments flashing at us every second of every day while we're still trying to manage life in the physical world. To handle this constant onslaught of information, our brains have to choose what to flag up to us and they do this via a system called 'thought processing'. You simply don't have time to examine the ins and outs of everything that happens to you, so you start doing some things on autopilot. For example, putting on your trousers. You don't talk yourself through every step of putting on your trousers: 'I'm going to pick up the trousers, lift up my right leg, put my foot in the leg-hole, pull up the trousers and so on'. You just do it; it's become automatic. This kind of information-filtering allows us to live at the pace we do. If we didn't have that ability, our brains would explode. (Probably not literally, but you never know.) Your brain only flags up the things it deems to be important. It's really pretty clever.

However, the cleverness falters when our brains only filter through the information it finds that validates our own beliefs – but this is the way we're designed. It's part of the 'confirmation bias' we have that causes so many tricky problems. It's very hard to change a strongly held belief. Why? Because we are programmed to look for things that support the way we think. We cherry-pick the evidence that proves that we are right and disregard that which doesn't. This means that when you're scared and your brain is frantically trying to work out what to flag up to you as worthy of notice, it will pick the things that back up this feeling. It will actively look for 'threats' and 'dangers'. It has been trained to pay attention to things that are consistent with the view that you can't cope.

Your brain's not doing this to be a massive jerk; it's doing it to keep you 'safe'. If you're scared of breaking up with your partner, your brain categorises the breakup as threatening and so looks for proof to back up that view, so you can stay out of 'danger'. It'll zoom in on articles that say being single sucks, Instagram pictures of happy couples or off-the-cuff comments from your partner about how he/she wouldn't cope without you. This inevitably influences your behaviour, by, for example, avoiding the issue, making excuses or blaming yourself or others for your feelings of frustration. This, in turn, triggers the fight or flight reflex whenever you think about it and you can kiss any rational assessment of the situation goodbye (see Chapter 3 for more on fight or flight).

Ⓢ Your fear mind map

Fill in a mind map focusing on a recent time you felt frightened. I'm asking you to focus on your fear, to relive something that provokes strong physical and emotional responses. That can be very tough to do, but starting to think about your own personal reaction to fear is an integral part of the process.

Often, an easy place to start is with the physical feeling of fear. When did your heart last start racing, your chest feel tight or your hands get sweaty? What were you thinking of at the time? How did these thoughts affect your mood and what did they cause you to do? I've included an example opposite, which doesn't include the 'event' box. With a more generalised feeling of fear, often it isn't just one event that triggers the feeling, so focus more on your thoughts, body, behaviour and emotions. Have a look back at the symptom checklist in Chapter 1 to trigger your memory if you need to. (If you do remember the event, by all means stick the event box back in the middle.)

While not exactly pleasant, thinking deeply about a specific fear will show you the knock-on effect of thoughts, emotions, behaviour and physicality. You can start seeing how they affect each other and can also see, hopefully, how changing one will cause the others to change in turn.

When you were filling out the mind map, where did you start?

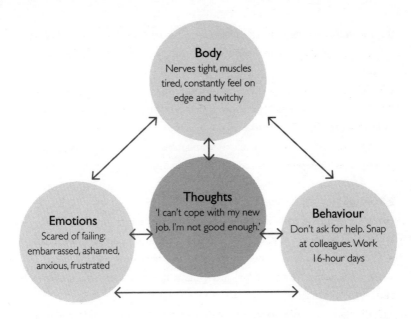

Recognising where you personally experience fear first will be helpful when it comes to interrupting negative patterns. You'll be able to think, 'I know this behaviour can lead to a drop in mood' or 'I know this thumping of my heart can lead to bad behaviour' and put in place the strategies you'll learn in this book for making changes. The more mind maps you fill in, the easier it will become to identify these patterns.

⑤ Changing your mind map

Using some of the knowledge you've acquired in this chapter, try to alter your fear mind map. Look for alternative interpretations to your fear, actively try to challenge your thoughts (remember THOUGHTS AREN'T FACTS!), assess different ways you could act – ways that would encourage more positive outcomes – and try to calm down your riled-up body. How do these changes then affect your mood? I've used the example in the previous mind map to give you some starting points:

Thoughts: I went through a rigorous interview process to get the job, so I must be qualified. Even if I'm not qualified, the people who gave me the job must have seen something in me that they liked. They believed in me, so maybe I should too. Of course, I won't know everything straight away – how could I? Asking for help is not a show of weakness.

Behaviour: It's not my colleagues' fault I feel overwhelmed. I shouldn't snap at them. That will only alienate them and make them suspect that I don't know what I'm doing. I'll act more calmly and pleasantly. I'll ask them to explain a few of the basics and how the structure of the company works. It'll please them that I've asked and will show I'm not stubborn. I'll also stop working such long hours. I'm not achieving anything except exhausting myself.

Body: I'm tired, run down and constantly on edge. This affects my decision-making capabilities and makes me appear unapproachable to others. I'll work at calming my body down using the strategies detailed in Chapter 3.

Emotions: Cross-examining my thoughts, acting in more positive ways and relaxing my body will all improve my mood as I'll feel more in control and therefore less afraid.

Thoughts to take away

✓ Your thoughts, body, emotions and behaviour are all linked. If one of these is negative, the rest will follow, just as if you change one to positive, the rest will change too

✓ When you feel scared, your brain actively looks for 'threats' and clutches on to 'proof' of the danger. You have to retrain your brain to look for alternative views that are fairer and more realistic

✓ THOUGHTS AREN'T FACTS. They can be challenged!

3

Panic Stations

The physical effects of fear are the most obvious and the most debilitating. You simply can't change your mindset when you're in fight or flight mode. This chapter will teach you how to calm down your body so you can feel more in control.

Am I having a heart attack?

You're hiding in the toilets at your best friend's wedding. It's nearly time for you to stand up in front of everyone and give the speech you've spent two months preparing. But you can't breathe. It feels as if an iron bar is being slowly tightened around your chest. Your heart is flapping like a trapped bird, your hands are shaking and you can't even feel your feet any more – they've gone numb.

'I'm having a heart attack!' you think. 'I'm going to drop dead on the toilet at my best friend's wedding and ruin her life.' The good news is, you're not having a heart attack. The bad news is, you might be having a panic attack. The best-case news is, you're probably in fight or flight mode.

The physical repercussions of fear are an absolute bastard, to put it nicely. They not only affect your body, but your mind too. You can't think straight when you're experiencing all the symptoms detailed on page 47 and so your assessment of your ability to cope gets screwed up. Also, what happens to your body is so dramatic that you can start to fear the physical act of fear itself. You dread going into fight or flight so much that you'll do anything to avoid it. Often, when people say, 'I can't deal with confrontation', 'I can't stand up for myself', 'I hate public speaking' or 'I can't leave her' what they actually mean is, 'I don't want to feel as if I'm having a heart attack'. This fear of fight or flight is how conditioned fears are born. You associate job interviews with sweaty palms and headaches, so you avoid them like the plague. You associate telling someone you're upset with having to sit on the floor with your head between your legs and so you avoid doing that too. All of which means you limit your opportunities and fail to make changes – without even thinking deeply about why. Certain things have been categorised as 'bad' in your head and you've just accepted that without ever challenging the definition.

What is this natural reflex, this thing we're all born with, that causes so much trauma?

Fight or flight

I mentioned fight or flight earlier in Chapter 1 because it's such an integral part of the whole fear experience ('the fear experience' sounds like a fairground ride, which, in a strange way, isn't too far off the mark), but here's where we're really going to pin it down.

Fight or flight is the physiological response to fear. It's an evolutionary kick-back from our cave-dwelling days, when we had to rely on our instincts to avoid being gored by a saber-toothed tiger near the fire-pit. Here's how it works. Imagine you're enjoying a peaceful swim in a beautiful lagoon. Ripples of water a little distance away attract your attention, but there's nothing and no one there. You carry on swimming. Suddenly there's a huge splash about 100 metres away. The surface of the water breaks and a sleek grey fin emerges. It starts cutting through the water straight towards you. Immediately your sympathetic nervous system floods your body with adrenaline and cortisol, making your heart beat faster to pump blood away from the places that don't need it to the muscles that do. This includes diverting it from your fingers and toes, which is why you may feel tingling and literally experience 'cold feet'. Digestion slows or stops, so you may feel, or be, sick. The blood vessels in your skin constrict to ward against excessive blood loss if you're attacked and you'll sweat more to stop overheating, making you look pale and clammy. You start breathing heavily to get more oxygen into your bloodstream and your sensory perceptions increase (your pupils dilating so that you can see more clearly and your hearing sharpening), while a rush of endorphins diminishes your perception of pain.

Fight or flight has turned you into a lean, mean fighting-or-fleeing machine. As such, the bits of your brain that deal with rational thought take a back seat, leaving your decision-making lobes in charge. Your brain doesn't want you to start pondering, 'What's the likelihood of there being a flesh-eating shark in this particular lagoon?' It knows that thoughts like that will only slow you down. Instead it simply screams, 'SWIM AWAY OR PUNCH IT ON THE NOSE!'

When you're in this state everything becomes a potential threat. If someone swam up behind you and patted you on the shoulder there's a strong chance you'd turn around and punch them on the nose instead. You'll overreact to the slightest provocation because, as far as your body is concerned, this is a life-or-death situation.

The fin gets closer and closer. You're desperately trying to see the shark through the water, but it's too murky. And then the fin disappears... All is quiet. You whip around, paddling desperately, eyes wide, heart hammering and then the fin reappears right in front of your face. You swing your fist backwards and... it's just a jolly dolphin! Playing games! The rascal! The relief at the danger passing causes your parasympathetic system to kick in, releasing noradrenaline, which reverses the changes, cooling and calming you down. The tension leaves your body and you smile weakly as the dolphin cackles in your face.

Now, that whole physical rigmarole sounds positively brilliant when you're facing a hungry shark. You want your body to be in survival mode then. But what about when the 'threat' is your furious mother-in-law shouting about the red wine you've spilled on her brand-new white carpet? A hammering heart, sweaty palms and constricted chest aren't ideal then. That's the problem with fight or flight: it hasn't evolved as quickly as our lives have. It's just as sensitive as it was when we were battling saber-toothed tigers and it's triggered whenever we feel fear or anxiety. Job insecurity, relationship problems or unpaid bills can't be resolved by fighting or running away, but your body preps you just the same. Also, it can't differentiate between unconditioned and conditioned fears, or corporeal problems and psychological ones. You can experience the same physical response facing a charging bull as you can facing a room full of colleagues waiting for you to present some work.

Another example is illustrated in this mind map:

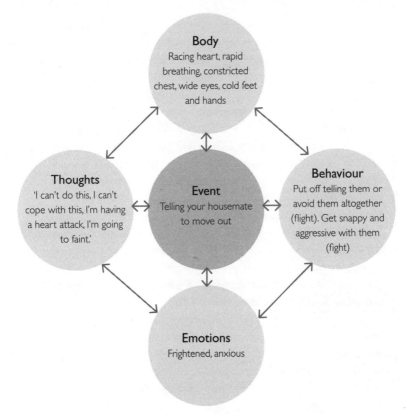

If your life is very stressful and you often feel overwhelmed, your fight or flight reflex can be activated all the time. So often, in fact, that your body doesn't get a chance to calm down properly. Living in a permanent state of tension can have both long-term physical consequences (i.e. nausea, constipation, insomnia, hot flashes, dizziness) and mental consequences (i.e. scattered thoughts, anger, defensiveness, inability to concentrate,

Why you 'freeze'

Freezing is an often-overlooked physical symptom of fear as it usually occurs before fight or flight kicks in. You'll freeze instinctively if you hear or see anything that your body interprets as potentially dangerous and often when you are surprised (your eyes will widen to better process your surroundings and your mouth will open in preparation to scream or breathe heavily as you run). By freezing you limit the distraction of changing visual and aural stimulus so you can focus fully on the 'threat'. Your body is giving your brain time to work out how much fear it should feel and whether it needs to go into fight or flight while also ensuring you provide less of a target to potential attackers by staying still. In the shark-attack example, you'd freeze when you heard the first splash and then again when you heard the second. It's only when you saw the fin that your body would go into full-blown fight or flight. However, if you feel completely overwhelmed, trapped or overpowered, and can neither fight or flee, your body can stay 'frozen', immobilising you. This is why some people seemingly don't react if they are threatened. Your primitive brain is making your body 'play dead' by freezing up in the hope the predator will lose interest and leave. When in this state your attentional systems can shut down so you don't process what is happening and so can't form memories of the event. It's the body's way of psychologically protecting you against trauma. Freezing is instinctual, so is usually only triggered by unconditioned fears (the perception of an immediate physical threat) rather than conditioned everyday fears, where anxiety can ramp up slowly over time.

a sense of disconnectedness). These can be exacerbated by the use of drink or drugs. One thing that won't happen, though, is fainting. You can't faint when you are in fight or flight as evolution is much smarter than that. It would be a pretty rubbish physical defence when faced with danger if you just collapsed to the floor. There are lots of other reasons why you might faint, but fight or flight isn't one of them. However, you can faint when faced with the sight of blood or guts. This is believed to be an evolutionary failsafe, as fainting lowers the heart rate and blood pressure in order to slow down blood loss if you're the one who is bleeding and also so you appear dead to your attackers. This form of playing dead would be kind of cool if we all still lived in 30,000 BC, but it's not so useful if you've just got a paper cut.

So, while fight or flight is a natural consequence of fear and you can't stop it happening completely (and you shouldn't want to, you need that response if you're ever faced with a shark or charging bull), the symptoms can be managed when you experience them over conditioned fears. Often we ignore the physical warning signs our body gives us, only realising we're in trouble when we're curled up in a corner breathing into a paper bag. Learning to recognise the signs will enable you to halt the effects before they hit full-throttle. And, if they do hit full-throttle, you'll know how to calm yourself down.

S Your fight or flight mind map

Fill in a mind map of a recent time when either fight or flight affected you or the fear of fight or flight affected you. What situation were you facing or thinking about facing? What happened to your body, what thoughts ran through your mind, how did you feel emotionally and what did this make you do?

Acknowledging how your body personally reacts to fear is the first step in making meaningful changes. You can't think rationally when you are in fight or flight – that's a fact. It's biology. You have to calm down your body to reignite your rational and logical mind. Only then can you start assessing the situation in an effective way. You can then also change your behaviour. When you're in fight or flight you're more likely to lash out, snap at people and behave defensively (fight) or hide away, clam up or revert to sarcasm as a masking device to hide your true feelings (flight). Any of that sound familiar? Write it down.

A word on panic attacks

A panic attack is a dramatic and sudden physical reaction to an intense feeling of fear. Basically, it's fight or flight supersized. Your body goes through everything I've previously described, but the symptoms progress to their most extreme levels very rapidly. Panic attacks can last for between five and twenty minutes. If the attack goes on for longer than this, you're probably experiencing one attack after another or are maintaining a high level of anxiety (fight or flight) after the initial attack. The worst thing about panic attacks is that they can often happen randomly, for no discernible reason, in the least convenient places.

Physical symptoms include:
+ An irregular or pounding heartbeat
+ Increased sweating
+ Trembling or shaking limbs, 'legs like jelly'
+ Feeling unable to breathe, hyperventilating
+ A tight throat, a feeling as if you're choking
+ Nausea
+ Dizziness
+ Ringing in your ears
+ Tingling fingers
+ Faintness

- ✦ Feeling as if you're not connected to your body
- ✦ Chattering teeth

Mental symptoms include feeling that:
- ✦ You've lost control
- ✦ You're going to faint
- ✦ You're having a heart attack
- ✦ You're going to die

Panic attacks can be absolutely terrifying, but the good news is: you're not having a heart attack, you're not going to faint and you're not going to die. Despite how intense they feel, panic attacks are not dangerous and won't cause you any physical harm, so you shouldn't go to hospital. Most people won't ever experience a panic attack, but many will. They can happen at times of extreme stress, one or two times a month or, in worst-case scenarios, several times a week. If this sounds like you, you should visit your doctor because you may be suffering from panic disorder. While the strategies in this book will help you in dealing with your fear, your doctor will be able to recommend more specialised treatment.

How to calm down your terrified body

These strategies will calm you down, both when you feel the first stirrings of fight or flight and when you're experiencing a full-blown physical meltdown.

Ⓢ Do a deep-breathing exercise

You can do this simple deep-breathing exercise anywhere.
1 Put one hand on your chest; one on your abdomen
2 Inhale deeply through your nose and out through your mouth
3 Count to five on the inhale and five on the exhale

4 Expand your abdomen on your inhale, so that it pushes up your hand

5 Feel your abdomen compress on your exhale

6 Continue doing this until your body feels more relaxed

Ⓢ Focus on something 'non-threatening'

Concentrate all your attention on something non-threatening. For example, your watch. What does it look like? Can you hear it tick? What does it feel like? Count the seconds as they pass. If you're not wearing a watch, look for something neutral around you – a poster, a book cover, a leaflet, a pair of shoes or an advertising hoarding. Pick out the colours or imagine what the textures feel like. Avoid focusing on anything personal (like photographs) or any technology that will alert you to new emails, social media updates, texts or phone calls. The last thing you want is to be reminded of a row you're having with your sister or see a text message ping up from your boss.

Ⓢ Sniff a happy-memory scent

When you know you are walking into a stressful situation, carry a bottle of scent with you that reminds you of a happy memory. Your olfactory bulb, which processes smell, is connected to areas of the brain that are strongly linked to emotion and memory. A strong sniff of a scent that reminds you of a good time can trigger happy memories that will help to calm you down, limiting anxiety and so stopping the advent of fight or flight.

Ⓢ Remind yourself that these emotions will pass

Feelings aren't permanent. You have felt happy and calm before and you will again. Tell yourself this. Repeat it over and over again, either out loud or in your head: 'Feelings aren't permanent. This will pass. I will feel calm again.' (See Chapter 6.)

⑤ Say to yourself, 'I am not dying'

As hideous as the physical repercussions of fear are, you can cope with them; they are not dangerous and you are not dying. Remind yourself of this – it can be easy to forget in the panic of the moment: 'I am not dying. This physical feeling isn't permanent. This too will pass.'

Thoughts to take away

✓ Fight or flight is the natural physical response to fear. By recognising the symptoms, you can learn how to calm your body down so you can assess the situation more rationally

✓ Fight or flight is not dangerous and the feeling will pass. Fear and anxiety go up… but then always come back down. So you will not feel this way forever

✓ Your thoughts are not logical or rational when you are in the midst of fight or flight, so don't automatically believe them!

4

Runaway Brain

That little voice in your head that tells you you're not good enough or that whatever you're planning will be a disaster can dictate the choices you make (or don't make). And the truth is, that little voice is chatting absolute rubbish. This chapter will teach you how to identify your inner critic – and then ignore it.

Meet your inner critic

Imagine I introduced you to 'a close friend' of mine and they proceeded to belittle me for the next three hours. Everything I said they contradicted or laughed at. And then they started on you. 'No, you're wrong', 'That's not what happened', 'Are you sure you did that? I don't believe you.' We both leave feeling low, insecure, angry and frustrated. Imagine, then, that I told you I'd invited that friend to move in with me. You'd be worried, right? Concerned for me? You might even say something like, 'Are you sure? They seem a little... critical. A little harsh.' Or you wouldn't say anything, figuring it wasn't any of your business. But either way, you'd have a strong opinion about it. And you'd definitely not want to hang out with that person again.

So why are you?

The person I've just described lives in your head. It's the little voice that tells you, 'You can't cope' or 'You're not good enough' and whistles through its teeth whenever you consider doing something a bit brave. The reason you don't treat this voice like you would my so-called friend – by distancing yourself from it, questioning it or showing it the contempt it deserves – is because you believe it. It's incredibly convincing, only ever spotlighting and seeming to confirm things you've long believed about yourself. For example, if you've always felt unlovable, your inner critic will focus on this inexhaustibly: 'He/she turned you down because everyone turns you down' or 'They treat you badly because you deserve it'. It also dismisses anything that disproves its theory, saying it 'doesn't count' somehow: 'She only asked you on a date out of pity'.

The worst thing about this critic is that it is so settled in your brain – sipping a whiskey with its feet up – that you don't even notice its vile outbursts any more. When thoughts like 'I'm too scared to do this' zip through your mind, you don't even hear them, you just accept them as facts. They relentlessly chip away at your self-esteem, both maintaining and aggravating your fears. Worse, they seem plausible (you may well be frightened), so you trust them. But they're never realistic (you can push through your fear – you have options). And, needless to say, they have a huge effect on your emotions, behaviour and body.

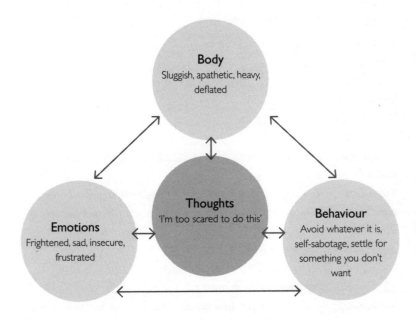

The responses detailed in the mind map are typical – and they please your inner critic immensely for they prove it right. Your body is saying, 'Yes, I'm terrified', your behaviour (avoidance or messing up on purpose) makes you think, 'I was right – this is too frightening', and your mood cloaks the whole endeavour in gloom. And all from the tiny little thought, 'I'm too scared to do this'.

The chief and the wolf parable (cheesy, but spot-on)

An old Cherokee chief was teaching his grandson about life. 'A fight is going on inside me,' he said to the boy. 'It is a terrible fight and it is between two wolves. One is evil – he is anger, envy, sorrow, regret, greed, arrogance, self-pity, guilt, resentment, inferiority, lies, false pride, superiority, self-doubt and ego. The other is good – he is joy, peace, love, hope, serenity, humility, kindness, benevolence, empathy, generosity, truth, compassion and faith. This same fight is going on inside you – and inside every other person, too.'

The grandson thought about it for a minute and then asked his grandfather, 'Which wolf will win?'

The old chief simply replied, 'The one you feed.'

The way to start changing how you think and feel about fear is to start noticing these thoughts as they whizz through your mind, not letting them flit in and out unchecked. You need to spot them and then slap them down with a fly swat like rogue bugs.

Ⓢ Fly-swatting your inner critic

For one day note down all your inner critic's statements – the negative thoughts that whizz through your mind automatically. Every single time you find yourself dismissing your abilities, criticising yourself, downplaying your achievements or telling yourself off, write down your thoughts and then fill in the rest of the table.

Seeing all the negative thoughts you have about yourself written down like this will probably be quite shocking. You'll hopefully be able to see how wildly unfair they are now that you've isolated them and examined them without the background hum of your anxious brain constantly

Your critical thought table

Critic's thought	What were you doing/ considering doing at the time?	Where were you?	How did this thought make you feel emotionally?	How did it affect your body?	How did it affect your behaviour?
'They're going to laugh at me'	Signing up at the gym	Standing outside the gym	Sad, pathetic	Hunched shoulders, thumping heart	I walked away and didn't sign up
'My flatmate hates me'	Asking my flatmate if I can watch what I want on TV occasionally	Watching what she wants on TV, as always	Furious, frustrated	Rigid posture, fluttery stomach, red face	I couldn't concentrate on the show and started snapping at her
'I can't be on my own'	Considering what I'd do if my husband died	Driving back from the hospital	Panicked, sad	Racing heart, short of breath, shaking hands	I had to pull the car over and take deep breaths

interrupting. Look at your list – these are things you think about yourself every single day. Pretty grim, eh? No wonder you feel scared.

Are several of your inner critic's thoughts about one thing in particular (e.g. your appearance, your fear of loneliness, your inability to progress in your career or your general sense that life has it in for you)? Do these thoughts often happen in the same place or with the same people? Is your resulting behaviour often the same (e.g. do you often isolate yourself, react aggressively or comfort eat?)? Note down any patterns. You may be surprised at what you discover – at the situations, people or places that are involved when you tend to be most harsh on yourself.

Categorising your inner critic's thoughts

Jot down the categories listed below in your notebook so that you become familiar with them. Then try to fit the thoughts from your critical thought table into each definition. Paying more attention to these kinds of thoughts – analysing them and holding them to account – is an essential part of feeling fearless. Understanding the games your mind is playing will make your thoughts lose their power so you'll be more inclined to seek alternative views.

Fortune-telling

Stuff like, 'This will be a disaster' or 'They'll all laugh at me'. Guess what? You're not a fortune-teller. Just because you think something will happen, doesn't mean it will.

Reading minds

'They're thinking I'm not good enough', 'They hate me'. How do you know? Have you asked? Then pipe down. You're not in X-Men, ergo, you can't read minds.

My emotions affect the whole world

'Everything's out to get me today'. No it isn't. Your moods and emotions cannot influence a planet. You are not a deity. Perhaps you're behaving in ways that invite negativity or you are only focusing on the bad things (ever noticed how we never go 'Hurray! The bus is on time!' only ever, 'Oh God, I can't believe the bus is late again'?). Just because you feel bad, doesn't mean it's bad (whatever 'it' happens to be at the time).

Catastrophising

'This is the worst thing ever! I will never get over this!' Come on – time for a little perspective, perhaps?

Black or white

It's wrong or right, a success or a failure, all or nothing, with no middle ground. Hey – there's *always* a middle ground.

Overgeneralising

'I *never* get promoted', 'I *always* get turned down', 'I *never* win any awards', 'I *always* mess up'. Shouldn't that be 'I sometimes mess up' or 'I didn't win this time'? Overgeneralising is characterised by the words 'never' and 'always'. So what if something doesn't go your way once or even twice? That doesn't mean that things can't change. Take what you've learned and move on.

It's all about me

'Typical! This always happens to me', 'Other people are so lucky', 'She always has to try to beat me', 'He never smiles at me'. Dude – not everything is about you. People are just busy getting on with their own lives. You are not the axis upon which all things spin. Sorry.

That doesn't count

'She only complimented me because she had to', 'I only did well because the better candidate didn't show up', 'I only look nice in that picture because of the light'. This is thought-filtering at its most damaging. You're choosing to dismiss evidence that proves you've done well or are succeeding because it doesn't fit your embedded belief system (and inner critic's warblings) that you're not good enough. You can't cherry-pick 'proof' this way. You need to start crediting yourself for your achievements and paying attention to compliments.

Starting to notice thought patterns like these (are lots of them about one thing and do many of them fall into into one particular thought category such as 'reading minds' or 'fortune-telling'?) is the first step in learning how to interrupt them. You can begin to see how they're all related to one particular aspect of how you view yourself and the world. And, hopefully, you'll start to realise that your view is an incredibly flawed, biased view. Now you're aware of your inner critic you'll know to look out for thoughts like these and won't just allow them to rampage through your head unchecked.

So, now you've swatted them, what next?

⑤ Criticise your critic

Put your critic's claims to the test. This is a development of the thought-challenge strategy in Chapter 2. The hardest bit to complete will be the section that asks you to find evidence both for and against the thought. You'll no doubt have zero trouble finding evidence to back up the thought that you won't be able to manage or that things will be awful, but finding evidence *against* the thought will be a lot tougher. To help remember to ask yourself, 'Is there another way to think about this – another opinion, a fairer one?' Also, 'Have I ever tackled something like this before?' And finally, 'What would I tell a friend in this situation?' We're always fairer to our friends than we are to ourselves.

Forcing yourself to find views that conflict your inner critic's will feel alien to you. You've accepted these thoughts as fundamental truths for a long time. But you're not doing anything radical – you're just trying to find a fair and balanced view based on the actual evidence of the situation. Your inner critic is not fair or balanced. The sooner you can accept that, the sooner it will feel natural seeking out evidence that backs up your strengths rather than your supposed weaknesses. Thinking of advice you would give a friend is a great way to get a more realistic perspective on

Criticising your critic table

Situation	Telling my best friend I think she drinks too much	Putting on weight
Critic's thought (also note the category of thought)	'She'll hate me for it' (fortune-telling)	'I'm fat and ugly and everybody thinks so' (reading minds)
How strongly do you believe this?	80%	100%
Emotion	Scared, anxious, frustrated	Embarrassed, ashamed
Behaviour	Put off telling her and act shifty whenever we're out drinking together	Say no to invitations out, wear dark, nondescript clothes
Body	Tense, ball of anxiety in stomach	Slumped, hunched-over
Evidence FOR the thought	No one would want to be told this! She'll get defensive and blame me. She'll think I'm being judgemental and snobby	I've put on two stone, so of course I'm now fat. And, of course, everyone will have noticed
Evidence AGAINST the thought: What is the fair view? Have you ever done something like this before? What would you tell a friend in this situation?	We've told each other tough things in the past and it's been okay. She'll get defensive but will know deep down I'm only saying it because I care. She's had blackouts recently – that's not something she can deny – so she'll know I'm not just being snobby, but worried	While people might have noticed, it doesn't mean they think I'm fat or ugly. I haven't actually asked them what they think. I'd tell a friend they were being really harsh. I don't actually think I'm ugly, just bigger. I've actually had a couple of compliments recently about how I look
How strongly do you believe the thought now?	40%	50%

the situation. We're always less compassionate to ourselves than we are to others. And if you would give that advice to your friend, it can't be total gubbins, can it?

Now you're getting into the swing of identifying these thoughts and weighing up the evidence for and against them, the next step is to try to stop your inner critic spouting them at all. To cheer them up; to make them less of a downer. And the way to do that is to break down their prejudice.

With extreme prejudice

Your inner critic is very prejudiced against you. They think you're pretty rubbish at stuff and will be pretty rubbish at stuff despite having no evidence to back it up. Because that's the thing about prejudice, it's a belief, and as with all beliefs, you don't need evidence, you just need faith that they're true. And, as you'll know if you've ever tried to argue with someone about a staunchly held belief, altering their mind is akin to banging your head against a breeze-block wall while poking yourself in the eye with a stick for good measure.

Imagine this: your dad is immensely prejudiced against female doctors and surgeons. So much so, in fact, that he refuses to be treated by a woman whether in hospital or at his local GP surgery. This has led to countless awkward situations and, actually, some pretty dangerous ones – particularly when his appendix burst and he still managed to cause a scene in A&E. You have told him a bajillion times that he is being offensive and old-fashioned. You have shown him stats, facts and papers explaining how his opinion is ludicrous, but it doesn't matter. You could talk to him until you're blue in the face. In fact, you could talk to him until you're so blue in the face that a female doctor has to come and save your life – and he still wouldn't change his mind. That doctor would be an aberration, an exception to the rule, someone who got lucky one time. The thing is – he doesn't *want* to know.

And neither does your inner critic. They like thinking you're not brave enough and you can't cope because it keeps things stable and safe. They don't want to rock the boat, so as soon as you even think about making changes, they'll slam on the brakes, screaming 'Woah, there! Calm down, chill out! You're not ready for that.'

To stop your inner critic's prejudice messing up your quest to become fearless, you need to open your mind to evidence that disproves what they say – to pay attention to things that debunk the theory that you're a bit crap. So, are you up for believing you can be brave and that you can cope with tough situations? The fact that you've picked up this book and read this far would suggest that, yes, you are. Congrats! That's a major step in shutting up that naysaying little voice in your head for good.

⑤ Three times you were brave

Copy down the table on page 68 in your notebook and think of three times in your life when you were brave – when you felt frightened, but did whatever it was you had to do anyway. They can be anything: maybe you spoke up in a business meeting, presented a paper at university, passed your driving test or asked someone out.

Don't measure these things against what other people might consider brave. This is purely personal. People are frightened by different things. For you, getting on a plane might be the height of bravery, yet for an air steward it's an everyday event. Yet that same air steward might be petrified of public speaking, while you actually enjoy it. There's no common denominator for bravery. Yeah, sure, leaping in front of a car to save a child is a brave thing to do by any standard – and if you've done that, for God's sake, write it down! – but don't dismiss the everyday stuff, the conditioned fears that eat away at us. Pushing through those is the bravest thing we do.

Once you've got your three, fill out the rest of the table.

Your bravery table

	Brave act 1	Brave act 2	Brave act 3
What I did (and when)	When I was 20 years old, I had an operation on my back that I'd been putting off for many years	Left my abusive girlfriend of seven years earlier this year	Drove on the motorway for the first time ever last year
What this consisted of	An eight-hour operation, six weeks' recuperation, a year's physiotherapy	Moving out of our shared flat, finding somewhere new to live, explaining to her family and mine that I'd left her	Having four sessions of therapy to examine my fear of driving on motorways, then actually getting out there and doing it
Why it was brave	Because I had to defer my third year of university. I was frightened I'd lose touch with all the friends I'd made and would fall behind in my studies	She had threatened to kill herself if I left. That threat kept me in the relationship for an extra three years. I was terrified I would be responsible for her death	I've been frightened of motorways for years – I didn't even like being a passenger in a car on one. But it was severely limiting my experiences, so I tried therapy
What happened? What did it change?	Lots of my friends stayed on in the city anyway, so we kept in touch. I made new friends on my course, but most importantly I felt much better physically	She didn't kill herself. She moved back home with her parents. They're trying to get her some help. I feel much happier – and for the first time in ages, I don't feel guilty for feeling happy	It's changed my life. I didn't expect it to have as big an impact as it has, but now I actually like driving on motorways. I've started taking road trips across the country for fun!
How did it make me feel emotionally?	Empowered. Relieved. Excited for the future. Proud	Guilty and ashamed at first, but then free – as if I'd got my life back	Independent, brave and liberated. It's also weirdly relaxing

⑤ Save up compliments

Another way to start fighting back against your inner critic is to save up compliments. When we're feeling low, scared or anxious we often dismiss the praise we receive and instead hoard up criticisms to beat ourselves over the head with (the 'that doesn't count' category of thinking). Force yourself to pay attention to compliments by writing them down in your notebook. Then, whenever you're feeling insecure, flick back and re-read them. Nothing is off the table. If someone says you made them laugh, write it down. If someone says they like your jumper, write it down. Writing compliments down will make them seem more 'official' in your mind, so you'll be forced to accept that they *do* count.

⑤ Make yourself a 'success' pinboard

Mark your successes by making a pinboard (a real-life cork board or a virtual Pinterest board) full of photos or reminders of your achievements. If you've received an award, take a snap and pin it up or upload it. If you get a new job, take a selfie as soon as you hear the news or write down the date and post these up. A photo or reminder of the day you left hospital, made your first speech, cycled to work for the first time – anything! And then take a snap of the compliment page you've made in your notebook and whack that up too. Look at this board whenever your inner critic starts mouthing off and say (either out loud or in your head): 'I have pushed through my fears in the past and achieved great things – and I will again'.

⑤ Reward yourself

Rewarding yourself when you've achieved something or been brave enough to make changes can really boost your self-esteem and lift your mood. It means you're acknowledging your progress and are paying attention to the good rather than just the bad. Going out with friends, having a relaxing bath or buying yourself those trainers you've wanted for months is a great way of paying yourself the attention you've been withholding for ages, giving yourself a much-deserved (and probably long-overdue) 'well done'.

Ⓢ Practise compassion

In the parable on page 60 there were two wolves battling inside the chief. At the moment you just have the one wolf – your inner critic – prowling the territory. You need to create a second one to battle the first – a more compassionate one. Creating and nurturing your compassionate voice sounds like airy-fairy drivel, but it's not. Speaking to yourself compassionately is one of the most important aspects of building self-esteem, beating anxiety and combating fear. When you feel low or insecure, you're much harder on yourself than is either fair or right. To create this compassionate, fair and kinder wolf (and then feed it), simply ask yourself:

+ 'Would I be friends with someone who spoke to me the way my inner critic speaks to me?'
+ 'Would I speak to my friend the way my inner critic speaks to me?'
+ 'Would I tell my children the things I tell myself I can and can't do?'

Your answers will inevitably be 'no' to each of these questions. It can be shocking to realise how harsh you are on yourself when you step back and look at things this way. Don't let your inner critic have free rein in your head. Make a commitment to build up and nurture a more compassionate voice – it's a key step in feeling fearless.

Thoughts to take away

✓ Actively look for the alternative view to your inner critic's
  – the more compassionate and fairer view. You would never
  speak to a friend the way your critic speaks to you so don't
  let them get away with it!

✓ Keep looking for, and accepting, evidence to disprove your
  prejudice against yourself and you'll soon start believing you
  can push through your fear

✓ You've overcome difficulties before and you've been brave
  before. You can, and will, do both again!

5

No Worries

Worrying is like always carrying an umbrella 'just in case'. It not only fuels your fear, but permanently prepping for the worst means that you miss out on the best bits of life. This chapter will teach you how to stop worrying and start living.

A worrying habit

Worry is one of the thought processes that lies behind fear. It's what happens when fear reaches the part of our brain that likes to make stuff more complicated. Once fear hits the cerebral cortex it knocks on worry's door and invites in memory, imagination, emotion and anticipation. Wahoo! What a party! You not only start imagining worst-case scenarios, but remember when you felt terrible in the past and start anticipating feeling that way again. All of which ramps up your anxiety about whatever it is you're worried about – then fight or flight kicks in, your rational brain leaves in a huff and all the worry gremlins throw a huge rave in your head.

Worry comes from a fear of vulnerability and powerlessness and, in turn, it actually provokes both these feelings. The more you worry, the more your thoughts focus on 'what ifs' and anxieties about the future – the more vulnerable and less able to cope you feel… and so the more you worry. It's a vicious circle (see opposite).

Three types of worry

1 Worries you can't do anything about

These are the thoughts that propel fears over which you have no control: 'I'm worried my girlfriend might get hit by a car as she rides her bike to work', 'I'm worried I might get mugged one day', 'I'm worried I might get food poisoning and die', 'I'm worried my friend might move away'. These are all things that happen *to* us rather than happen *because* of us.

2 Worries you can do something about

These are the thoughts behind fears that you can control, such as, 'I'm worried about having kids. Will I be able to cope with the responsibility?' or 'I'm worried about failing my exam'. These things happen because of us, because of the choices we make. For example, you can choose whether

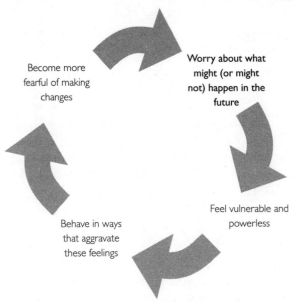

Worry about what might (or might not) happen in the future

Feel vulnerable and powerless

Behave in ways that aggravate these feelings

Become more fearful of making changes

or not to have kids and how to raise them, just as you can choose to revise more thoroughly for your exam.

3 'What ifs'

These little swines should be booted out of your head immediately. Stuff like, 'What if my sister shouts at me? What if I get fired? What if a piano falls on my head?' 'What ifs' like to make guest appearances in both categories 1 and 2 and they also prompt worst-case scenarios.

Why do we worry?

Studies are ongoing into the biology of worry, but there are indications that some people may be born with a susceptibility to anxiety and pessimism. They may be more likely to ruminate on the past and worry about the future. They may also have been brought up to worry by an anxious or over-careful parent. Or it may be neither of these things, but

Worry about worry

People can also worry about worrying. While many of us will sometimes think, 'I'm driving myself crazy! I need to stop worrying,' if this concern becomes genuine, i.e. if you actually believe worrying might be driving you crazy and are now worrying incessantly about that possibility, this can be a symptom of generalised anxiety disorder (GAD). GAD is a constant nervousness and anxiety about anything and everything, everyday matters, to such an extent that it dramatically inhibits your life. If this sounds like you, please see your doctor about further treatment.

down to an on-going issue in life that causes great unease. People can also believe that worrying is positive for any of the below reasons:

+ Worrying keeps me and others safe
+ It makes me prepare for all the worst possible outcomes
+ It means I care
+ It'll mean I can cope better if the worst happens

Contrary to popular belief WORRYING DOES NOT AFFECT A SITUATION'S OUTCOME. What you *do* affects the outcome – your behaviour. Your thoughts can't positively or negatively affect how something pans out. This is important. Many people think that worrying about something will help them to cope, to prepare for any eventuality or to prevent bad things from happening. Worrying doesn't help you to do any of those things. It merely ramps up your anxiety and fear so that you lose perspective and can't think rationally. Then fight or flight punches you in the gut and you physically can't make logical or reasonable assessments of the situation.

You need to catch worries, stamp on them before they make mayhem, and then analyse the situation without them buzzing around your head.

'What ifs' and worst-case scenarios

We're starting with 'what ifs' because they're the most recognisable.
Everyone thinks 'what if' on a fairly regular basis. It's how you act upon
the following thought that determines how much damage it causes. 'What
ifs' are contagious, with one leading to another and another, each building
and building on the last until soon you're worrying about something that
bears absolutely no resemblance to the original concern (and often no
resemblance to reality).

Example: What if the worst happened to Amy?

Dave was trying to call Amy, his girlfriend. They'd had a row on Thursday
night and he'd been trying to apologise all day Friday, but she wouldn't pick
up. It was now Saturday morning and her phone went straight to voicemail.
'What if she's still mad at me?' he thought. 'What if she doesn't forgive me?
What if she's met up with her ex? What if he wins her back? She wouldn't
turn her phone off though… Oh no! What if she's lost her phone? What if
she's been mugged? What if the mugger hurt her? What if she's in hospital?
What if she's been murdered?'

Dave's 'what ifs' cause him to plummet down a panic hole so deep he loses
all sense of reality. He's imagining his girlfriend fighting off murderers
when she's actually just left her phone at home and gone to stay with a
friend. In an hour, when she gets back, he'll get a text from her and all his
heart palpitations will have been for nothing.

Worst-case scenarios can play out as incredibly realistic visualisations,
like a film scene starring you or whoever you're worried about. This makes
even the most ridiculous imaginings seem very real. If you *see* yourself
falling off a stage, being slow-clapped out of a room or losing a limb

while skiing, even though you're only seeing it in your imagination, you'll believe it's realistic, possible – even likely, no matter how absurd it actually is. While you inhabit this visualisation you experience all the emotions you would if the thing was actually happening – you feel the shame, embarrassment, shock, anxiety, horror or anger. All of which tap into your inner-most fears and this fear spreads like a crack in ice. But you're not being scared about something that's real, but rather a totally made-up scenario you've just invented on the spot. But guess what? You're not a magician. Just because you think something will happen, that won't make it happen, otherwise we'd all be billionaires swigging rum on our yachts.

When you're feeling fearful 'what ifs' only ever lead to worst-case scenarios, never best-case scenarios. You never think: 'What if they're buying me a present? What if they're planning a huge surprise? What if they're booking me a wonderful holiday? What if they're going to tell me I've won the lottery!?' We only ever indulge the grim stuff. Which sucks. So, the next time you start imagining death and destruction raining down on your head, you need to get some perspective. Here's how:

⑤ What's *realistically* the worst that can happen?

Copy down this table in your notebook with a current 'what if' that is aggravating you. Allow the 'what if' to progress along its natural panicky channels. Let one lead to another – as they inevitably do. Write them all down until you get to your worst-case scenario. Then ask yourself, 'How much do I believe this?' How does this belief affect your mood, body and behaviour? Then try to combat this belief, finding proof against the thought: Is this logical? Is this actually likely? If a friend told you this, what would you say? Now, what is *realistically* the worst that might happen? And then, finally, how much do you believe the thought now?

Your worst-case scenario table

Situation	'What if Tim was upset when I made that joke about his black eye?'	'What if going travelling is a massive mistake?'
What's your worst-case scenario?	'What if he was lying when he said he'd got the black eye playing rugby but actually someone attacked him? What if he hates me for being insensitive? What if he never talks to me again? What if no one ever talks to me again?'	'What if I hate it? What if I don't make any new friends? What if, when I come back, I don't get as good a job as the one I've left? What if I return home to no friends, no job and no prospects?'
How strongly do you believe this? (0–100%)	80%	70%
Emotions	Anxious, guilty	Anxious, vulnerable
Body	Uptight	Nauseous, heart racing
Behaviour	Avoid Tim when I next see him	Put off travelling
If a friend told you this, how would you reassure them?	Tim's hardly over-sensitive about things, is he? Also, no one else who heard the joke reacted badly – everyone laughed! He probably has absolutely no idea why you're avoiding him	If you don't like it you can just come home. And you'll meet loads of new people plus you hated your job anyway – why would you want another like it?
Now reassess what realistically is the worst that might happen	If Tim did lie about how he got the black eye, he may have been sensitive about the joke – but he'd know it was an innocent remark and wouldn't blame me. I can apologise and we can both move on	I won't like some places I go to – but I'll love others. There's no way, with the right attitude, I won't enjoy myself. And, sure, I might not find the 'perfect' job when I come home, but I can keep looking
How much do you believe the original thought now? (0–100%)	15%	10%

Filling out this table will show you how quickly 'what ifs' can launch you face-first into Horror Fantasy Land, yet we rarely ever consider the question, 'What's *realistically* the worst that could happen?' We just indulge the hideous fantasies and freak out. The thing is, though, even if the realistic worst did happen, you'd be able to cope with it. Even if Tim was annoyed, you could just apologise and move on. Even if you did hate travelling, you could just come home. Saying to yourself, 'Hang on. Is that realistic? What's the worst that could happen, really? And could I cope with that?' will save you so much angst and pain.

How to stop worrying about stuff you do and don't have any control over

You can waste your entire life torn up with anxiety about what fate, circumstance or blind luck has in store for you. You can also waste your life worrying over future decisions you may or may not make (and the ramifications of both). Or you can get out there and live your life! When you next find yourself biting your nails while staring into space, work your way through the Worry Tree.

⑤ The Worry Tree

Just working through the Worry Tree opposite will make your anxiety about the issue drop naturally because you're taking action and being proactive. You're not letting worries swamp you. You decide that either there is something you can do about it, or there isn't; that you either do have some control over it or you don't. If you do have control over it, make a plan and then let your worry go. If you don't have any control over it, just let your worry go. In order to do that in both cases, you need to change the focus of your attention by following the strategies on page 82.

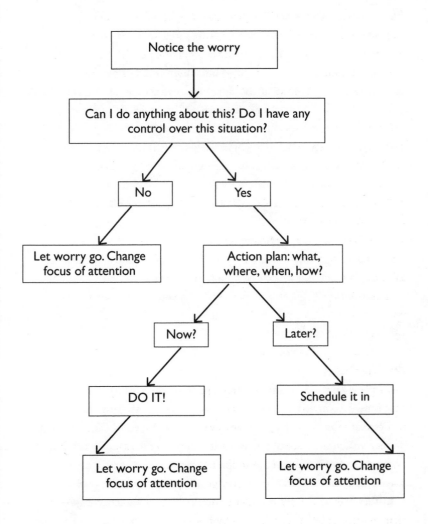

ⓢ Letting your worry go

A great way to learn how to view your thoughts abstractly, so you can get some distance from them, is to picture them as sentences printed on the sides of balloons. This is going to sound a little odd, but bear with me. Each worry floats past, gently bobbing on the breeze. You stand below and watch. 'I'm worried I won't get the job' wafts past. Next, 'I'm worried I'll never find someone to settle down with'. You observe them as an outsider, dispassionately, seeing them for what they are – simply thoughts, not facts or fortunes; streams of words that have no effect or power over you, unless you let them. You can now choose whether or not to engage with them. Do you want to grab the string of one of the balloons or do you want to let it float on by?

This exercise takes the power out of your worries. You can see how they come… and then go. How, without your interaction, they lose their potency. The balloons keep coming just as your new thoughts keep coming and they hopefully become more positive as you feel more in control.

ⓢ The rules of distraction

Once you've decided you can and will let your worry go, you need to distract yourself, otherwise they'll creep back in. Here's how:

1 Don't get angry at yourself for worrying (i.e. 'I can't believe I'm worrying about this – what's wrong with me?'). Worrying can be an ingrained coping mechanism you've relied on for years. Change will take time. Simply notice the thought (simply see the balloon) and then choose to think about something else (choose not to grab the string).

2 Distract yourself: read a book (and make sure you actually read it – if you reach the end of the chapter and can't remember anything about it, you're not distracting yourself successfully), play a game, do some work, watch a box set or call your friend. Anything to take your mind off your worry. Keep yourself busy.

3 Schedule in time to worry. Book a 15-minute slot into your diary in the evening. Then, when worries appear during the day, jot them down in your notebook and remind yourself that you're going to deal with them later. Knowing you're not ignoring them will make you worry less and often, by the time the scheduled time comes around, whatever you were worrying about has already been resolved or just doesn't seem that important any more.

Admit that worrying isn't positive

By this stage hopefully you can see why previously held beliefs that worry is in some way positive or beneficial are gibberish. Worry actively holds you back from making positive decisions, scrambling up your mind and freaking out your body. It does not keep you safe, it just sets a fire under your fears and warms them up nicely. If you want more proof, try the next two strategies:

ⓢ Is worrying positive? A pop quiz

Ask yourself the following questions:

+ Is worrying making me feel better or worse?
+ Is my worrying making other people feel better or worse?
+ Is worrying helping me make a rational plan for dealing with the issue?
+ Are there better, more positive ways of showing I care?
+ Does thinking up worst-case scenarios make me feel better or worse?
+ Does worrying make me always look for problems?
+ Does it make me feel pessimistic?
+ Does it make me try to influence others to think pessimistically?
+ Does it make me feel more apprehensive and fearful?
+ Does it make me feel tired, run-down and exhausted?

Answering these questions should prove that rather than being positive, worrying is actually incredibly debilitating, affecting both you and others in a negative way.

⑤ Give yourself a worry budget

If you find yourself chewed up by worries about everyday things (including 'what ifs'), give yourself a budget of ten worries a day. Are you going to waste one worry on whether your neighbour heard you arguing with your partner last night? If you are, remember you'll have one less to spend on wondering whether you were obnoxious at that party on Saturday… What's it going to be? In her book, *The Life-Changing Magic of Not Giving A F**k*, Sarah Knight advocates giving yourself a 'f*** budget'. The book is based upon the belief that caring less about things that really don't matter frees up your mind to focus on the stuff that actually does. And, as long as you're kind, honest and polite to people, you don't have to worry about offending them. This makes a lot of sense to me.

The point of this is not to actually ration your worries (because all worries are pointless), but to make you realise how futile they are. By forcing yourself to pick and choose them, you'll actually have to step back and analyse them dispassionately. You'll no doubt find that your ten worries dwindle to five and then, hopefully, to none as you realise that a) you don't care, b) it doesn't matter, or c) it does matter so you'd be far better off taking action than worrying any further.

When you're divvying them up, consider this: research by Dr Robert L. Leahy found that 85 per cent of worries have a neutral or positive outcome. And, regarding the other 15 per cent, 79 per cent of people studied reported that they handled the situation much better than they thought they would. In other words, they overestimated the danger and underestimated their ability to cope. It's as French Renaissance philosopher Michel de Montaigne said, 'My life has been full of terrible misfortune; most of which never happened'.

Thoughts to take away

✓ 'What ifs' are not only a total waste of time, but make you live through awful things in your head that most likely won't ever happen. And if they do happen, you'll be able to cope with them

✓ If you can't do anything about your worry, make a conscious decision to let it go and then distract yourself

✓ Worrying is not positive, beneficial or productive – making plans and taking action is

6

Look Who's Talking

You can't banish emotions. You can't get rid of them. They all serve a purpose. Accepting that fear is totally natural and something that will both come and go throughout your life is a huge part of feeling brave enough to face situations that scare you.

Hello fear, goodbye fear

Emotions are how you, as a human, process what's happening to you. They're how you work out what you like, dislike, want, don't want, fear or relish. They're also how you communicate and empathise with others (for example, sadness moves you and others to console and comfort each other). Your emotions affect your thoughts, behaviour and body in countless ways. It's all connected. Which is why learning how and why you feel the way you do about certain things is an essential step in discovering the best ways to change how you, personally, manage situations that give you the jeepers.

Before we go any further, there are a few truths you need to accept regarding your feelings.

Truths about emotions and fear

Truths about emotions

✦ We are designed to experience every emotion there is – everything from air-punching euphoria to hair-pulling sadness. You can't banish an emotion. You must accept fear as a natural consequence of being human

✦ Emotions are transient, not permanent. By their very nature they will come... and go. You will not feel fearful forever, just as you will not feel happy forever. Attempting to never feel frightened again is as fruitless as attempting to only ever feel happy

Truths about fear

✦ Fear is a perfectly natural response to doing something new

✦ There is nothing 'wrong' with you for feeling afraid

Write these points down in your notebook so that whenever you feel overwhelmed by one particular emotion, you can flick back, read them and feel reassured.

We can push our emotions away, try to ignore them or let them swallow us whole – particularly emotions we think of as 'bad', but fear is necessary. That is the fundamental lesson on which everything else is based. It's how you deal with fear that will determine the effect it has on your life.

Emotional flavours

Imagine that every emotion you experience has a 'flavour'. As with all foods, some taste good, some taste bad and some taste bland (neutral).

Good flavours: pleasant emotions that you enjoy experiencing
Bad flavours: unpleasant emotions that you don't enjoy experiencing
Neutral flavours: emotions that don't affect you much either way

Naturally, you gravitate towards the flavours that taste great – flavours like happiness and excitement. And, equally naturally, you try to veer away from the ones that taste terrible – flavours like sadness, grief, loneliness and rejection. You can hate these flavours so much that you come to fear tasting them. When you do get a mouthful, you either:

+ Try to 'fix' the feeling (do things to try to make the feeling 'better')
+ Ignore it
+ Wallow in it
+ Stop doing things that might cause you to taste it again

All of these strategies are rubbish. You can't 'fix' a feeling. Your emotions are there to help you interpret and navigate through your experiences. If something makes you feel scared, it's because you're scared. It's not a mistake. You can't act your way out of it. You have to accept the emotion and push through it. Attempting to ignore 'bad' emotions will only make them 'taste' worse as you prolong your discomfort. Wallowing in them will make you feel sad and even depressed, and staying within your comfort zone in an attempt to not feel it again will severely limit your experiences.

'Bad' emotions are as important to human experience and development as 'good' emotions. They teach you about yourself, about other people and enable learning and growth to take place. Without the 'bad' emotions you'd never truly appreciate the 'good' ones. The 'bad' flavours are healthy. They're good for you. You have to taste them occasionally.

Ⓢ What emotional flavours are you tasting?

Fill out a mind map with a recent situation where you felt fearful, anxious, stressed or upset, paying careful attention to the emotions section. I have re-included the list of common emotions associated with fear from the symptom checklist in Chapter 1 to help you. Include every emotion you felt in the lead-up to, during and after this event. It's all too easy to both experience and remember experiencing an event as simply making you feel 'bad', grouping all of your negative emotions together as one horrible flavour. This strategy will force you to pick apart the individual ingredients that make up the flavour to help you get to the bottom of what you're actually scared of.

Emotions to consider including:

✦ Fear	✦ Frustration
✦ Anxiety	✦ Anger
✦ Panic	✦ Defensiveness
✦ Guilt	✦ Sensitivity
✦ Shame	✦ Feeling overwhelmed
✦ Insecurity	✦ Feeling depressed

Isolating your emotions like this will give you more options for making changes. For example, in the situation shown in the mind map, you may not have realised that you not only felt angry about how this person treats you, but also insecure about it. Why insecure? What are you actually scared of? That you may have provoked their behaviour in some way? Also, the word 'frustrated' in the Emotions circle is interesting. Let's work through this new information.

- ✦ Where does your feeling of frustration come from? Do you feel you have no options in this situation because you 'can't cope with confrontation' so you have to put up with it? This thought seems to have triggered the whole situation, so let's analyse it
- ✦ Is the thought a fact? Let's weigh up the evidence for and against it. When have you dealt with difficult situations successfully before? How do you know it's going to be a confrontation at all – are you a fortune-teller? Are there ways you can negotiate the conversation so that it's non-confrontational? Are you going to spend your whole life feeling frustrated, defensive, angry and anxious whenever you're faced with difficult situations?
- ✦ What advice would you give a friend in this situation?
- ✦ Is your behaviour helping or hindering your ability to look at the issue in a rational way? Is it aggravating or calming your emotions?
- ✦ Consider why the person might be treating you in this way. Most people don't act badly for no reason. Could it perhaps be their own insecurity? Remember, you only have one side of the story. Ask them for their side. This will help with your own feelings of defensiveness and insecurity. Getting all the facts will stop your worst-case scenario thoughts as you'll know what you're dealing with

Analysing your mind map in this way will force you to look at the problem objectively, giving you some much-needed distance from it, enabling you to take action. And the fact that you're being proactive in thinking about the issue (rather than avoiding it) will defuse that feeling of overall 'badness'.

The problem with words like 'confrontation' and 'argument'

The words 'confrontation' and 'argument' are provocative. As in the example mind map, do you ever find yourself saying things like, 'I can't speak to her because I can't deal with confrontation' or 'I can't face an argument'? You're pre-empting the fact that you're about to have a row, which you can't possibly know for sure because you can't see into the future. This fear will lead you to putting off dealing with important issues. Sure, if you're about to tell someone something critical, you might get a defensive response (you also might not – something we rarely, if ever, consider). However, by bracing yourself in the expectation of having an argument, you're likely to approach the conversation in ways that make it argumentative, for example, by launching in aggressively as a defence mechanism. These kind of thoughts ramp up your anticipatory anxiety: 'She's going to shout at me so I'll get in with a zinger first', making it more likely that you WILL have a confrontation.

Swap the words 'confrontation' and 'argument' with 'conversation' and you'll reduce the anxiety you feel over the difficult chat you face so you can view the situation more calmly: 'I'm about to have a conversation' versus 'I'm about to have a confrontation'. It really makes a difference to how you view your ability to cope and how you'll then approach the chat.

Situational and personal mood triggers

The next stage is to identify the situational and personal triggers for your mood. When you've filled out mind maps, think about which section you have found the easiest to start with – your body, thoughts or behaviour? This is your 'personal trigger', while the event that kick-started the whole thing is the 'situational trigger'. Identifying both the personal and situational triggers will make you more aware of what's likely to happen when you encounter a tough situation again. Fear can snowball, making you forget what you were originally frightened of. Tracing things back to the beginning will give you some perspective on the issue as a whole and make you feel better able to make changes.

Situational trigger: What was the situation or event (real or imagined) that prompted the feeling?

Personal trigger: What triggered your mood – a thought, an action or physical feeling?

⑤ Identifying your mood triggers

Fill in the table for a recent event that made you experience a 'bad' mood flavour, trying to identify both the situational and personal triggers. I've filled out some examples to help.

Your mood-trigger table

Mood	Situational trigger	Personal trigger
Anxious	My landlord told me he wanted to sell the flat I rent	I felt a ball of heat rush through my body (physicality)
Angry	My friend told me he'd got the job I'd also applied for	I thought, 'What? They think he's better than me?' (thoughts)
Rejected and hurt	A guy I'd been dating stopped texting me back	Cancelled meeting my friend and stayed in (behaviour)

Acknowledging these triggers can help you to identify patterns in the future. For example, the next time you're talking to your landlord you can watch out for the symptoms of fight or flight. Or when you're next dating someone, you can be aware of times you're tempted to cancel evenings out with friends because you're anxious about how the relationship is going.

It's another step in learning how you personally deal with fear so you'll have more options for making changes in the future.

Guilt and shame: two of the worst-tasting emotional flavours

Many of our conditioned fears have their roots in guilt and shame, yet we often use the terms interchangeably, not realising the essential difference between the two. Understanding this difference is key to accepting your emotions and learning how to push through them.

The difference between guilt and shame

Guilt: An awareness that our actions have injured someone else
Shame: A judgement upon our own self-worth

So, in a nutshell:

Guilt: Doing something wrong
Shame: Being essentially wrong as a person, i.e. your core self is 'wrong'

You can feel both guilty and shameful about the same event. For example, Josh was at a party. He could see that his friend was getting on well with a woman who he himself quite fancied. He started taking the mick out of his friend in front of the woman. The more embarrassed his friend became, the more Josh ribbed him for 'not being able to take a joke'. In the end the woman left and his friend stormed off. Josh felt immediately guilty because he knew he had hurt his friend, but he also felt ashamed because he hadn't realised he was the kind of person who would act in that way.

The low-down on guilt

Guilt is an emotional warning sign learned in childhood. You were told off when you made another kid cry so you'd feel guilty as a way of learning wrong from right. It's how you developed empathy. Guilt also prompts you to examine your behaviour so you don't make the same mistake twice.

How to recognise guilt and use it effectively

There are two flavours of guilt and one of them actually is unhealthy. The trick is to know when you're scoffing that one rather than the healthy version.

Healthy guilt

When guilt causes you to re-evaluate your behaviour in a positive way that will improve your life. Healthy guilt impels us to repair important relationships and/or our own self-esteem.

Unhealthy guilt

When your behaviour doesn't need to be changed. For example, if you're a new mum and need/want to go back to work, but feel guilty about leaving your child. This kind of guilt serves no rational purpose and is usually caused by familial or societal expectations ingrained while growing up. You believe there is a certain way 'to be' and behaving differently will engender disapproval.

Ⓢ Is your guilt healthy or unhealthy?

Ask yourself:

1 Am I hurting, or have I hurt, anyone else?

+ No. Forget it, then. It's unhealthy guilt. Move on and consider reassessing your rules regarding acceptability and achievement

+ Yes. This is healthy guilt (it's justifiable). Go to question two

2 Do I want to change what I'm doing?

+ No. Is there a compromise to be made? Is it a case of misunderstanding? If you explained yourself might that help? Are you just being stubborn or selfish?
+ Yes. Then take action to change it

Healthy guilt won't go away until you make changes. Until the lesson is learned it'll keep returning like a boomerang.

Example: Healthy versus unhealthy guilt

Angela worked from home and chose her own hours, yet always felt incredibly guilty for watching telly in the middle of the day. She asked herself:

1 Am I hurting or have I hurt anyone else?
No.

She realised that this was unhealthy guilt, prompted by the societal expectation that working hours are 9am–5pm. The fact that she worked better in the evenings made her feel as if she was breaking some kind of external 'rule', so she felt guilty. This was nonsense.

However, she also felt guilty about the fact that she was dating a married guy. She did the same strategy for this issue too.

1 Am I hurting or have I hurt anyone else?
Yes.

2 Do I want to change what I'm doing?
No. Is there a compromise to be made? Is it a case of misunderstanding? If you explained yourself might that help? Are you just being stubborn or selfish?

⋯⋰

⋯⋰⋱

This forced her to really confront her guilt. She was potentially hurting her boyfriend's partner if they found out about the affair – and she clearly cared about this because she felt guilty (so it was healthy guilt). But she didn't want to leave him. She realised that until she made changes this guilt wouldn't go away and it was tainting the relationship. Could she live with the guilt and carry on as things were or did she need to speak to him about how she felt? For the first time in months she admitted that she couldn't ignore the feeling any more.

The shame game

Shame is the emotion that accompanies your inner critic's thoughts that you are somehow defective, inadequate, not up to scratch or just plain wrong inside. You will have learned shame from a very young age, either having been told you weren't good enough outright by parents or peers, or through how you were treated if you were given the impression you were a disappointment. This learning will have trailed you through adulthood and can be triggered by a more recent event or from generalised low self-esteem.

Shame can be considered the most disturbing emotion we will ever experience because it suggests that there is a problem with our 'self', our true being. Whatever makes us us is flawed in some way. How awful is that?

This feeling can manifest itself in damaging behaviours – eating disorders, alcoholism or drug addiction, for example – as you try to run from the emotion or mask it. But these actions just make you feel more ashamed. Hello, vicious circle!

One of the most common misconceptions about shame is that if you feel it you must have done something shameful. This simply isn't true. Shame is intrinsically connected to mid-level fears of humiliation, vulnerability, failure, rejection and disapproval. And, as you'll hopefully acknowledge by now, many of our judgements about what will cause us to experience those feelings are flawed because they come from our inner critic. And our inner critic is a total arsehole.

Why you feel ashamed

+ When your expectations or hopes are frustrated or blocked
+ A perceived failure
+ Lack of interest from others or negative interest from others
+ When your actions go against your core values

Why we can choose to hold on to shame

As strange as it sounds, we can choose to hold on to shame, almost revelling in it, without realising. We do this for several reasons:

1 Shame stops us making tough decisions because we 'don't deserve' change or success. People with very low self-esteem can feel as if they don't deserve good things to happen to them.

2 We can use shame to excuse bad behaviour: 'I did it because I'm a terrible person'.

3 Shame gives us a feeling of control over other people's feelings and behaviour. Our lack of control over other people's decisions and actions can make us feel helpless. And we hate feeling helpless. So, choosing to believe that it's all down to you – that it's your inadequacy making people behave in a certain way – gives you a feeling of being in control.

4 Shame makes us feel more in control of our own feelings. The belief that there is something intrinsically wrong with us can take the pressure off having to face up to grief, heartbreak, sadness, guilt and helplessness. If you insist on believing that someone's death was your fault, it relieves the burden of having to face the fact that sometimes really bad shit happens and there's nothing you can do about it. Thinking, 'If I had

done something different, that wouldn't have happened' makes you feel less helpless. The lack of control we have over the world and other people is often the most terrifying reality we have to face. Shame covers all of this up – but at a huge cost.

5 We can get used to feeling ashamed. If we were constantly told as a kid that we weren't good enough, we can hunt out situations that will induce these same feelings as adults, for example seeking out and staying in abusive relationships. If praise, comfort and kindness feel alien, uncomfortable and untrustworthy, we'll stick with what we know and what's familiar.

When shame makes you punish yourself and envy others

Holding on to a feeling that you are essentially flawed and so therefore don't deserve happiness and that everything is directly affected by you personally (including other people's actions and decisions) is a very self-involved way of living. It can also prompt extraordinary levels of self-chastisement. You forget or brush over the fact that other people have free will and that you can't control their thoughts or actions – e.g. you are not making a partner abusive; they are doing it of their own free will. This habit of personalising events can also give rise to an idealisation of other people's lives: 'They don't have to deal with what I have to deal with. They were dealt a better hand.' Or you can denigrate their achievements as being down to 'luck': 'She only got that job because she's lucky. Good things always happen to her.' This can turn to envy, an essentially selfish emotion, and if you then take action to hurt that person you'll be adding guilt into the mix too.

Shame is only useful when it prompts you to change your behaviour because whatever you're doing conflicts with your core values. If you believe in fairness, loyalty, honesty, a good work ethic and kindness, but are acting in ways that go against these beliefs, you will feel ashamed. Learning from your mistakes and acting differently will alleviate the shame you feel. However, punishing yourself, wallowing in it, martyring yourself, not learning from it and doing it again, obsessing over it or trying to 'fix' it, will only make the feeling grow. You have choices. No really, you do. You're not different, you're not flawed – you need to start choosing how you respond to events.

ⓢ Do you feel ashamed?

Fill in the table with a recent event that made you question yourself and how you'd behaved. I've filled out some examples.

The shame table

Event/situation	Drank too much at my friend's wedding	I skipped my driving test
Thoughts	'She doesn't want me here anyway'	'I'm so bad at driving – I'll probably kill someone'
Emotions during	Anger	Fear
Emotions afterwards	Guilt, shame and hurt	Guilt, shame and fury at myself
Behaviour afterwards	Laughed about it to other people but avoided my friend	Called my driving instructor to apologise. Made up some excuse about why I'd missed it and re-booked
Physicality (where did you feel the shame in your body)	In my face. Whenever I think about it I blush beet-red	In my throat. I found it hard to swallow

How to combat shame

Working through the shame table will hopefully have flagged up how your behaviour is influenced by feelings of shame and how issues can snowball if you let them. In the wedding example, by ignoring her friend, the person experiencing the shame has only piled on more things to feel guilty and ashamed about. The longer it goes on, the more frightened they'll become of rejection, humiliation and judgement.

Your actions in dealing with your emotions will dictate how things progress. They'll either get worse or get better. In the driving-test example, the person who skipped the test decided that the guilt they felt was healthy and so they took positive action to remedy this. They used the shame they felt to positive effect: 'I don't want to be the kind of person who doesn't value others' time, so I'll call and apologise.'

Running from your emotions, trying to 'fix' them, ignoring them or acting in ways that only exacerbate them ensure you keep thinking of them as 'bad'. They're not bad. They are your way of understanding your experiences. You may not enjoy feeling them, but you are feeling them for a reason. Accepting that is a fundamental part of living a better life. Remember that emotions pass. They are not frightening in and of themselves. They are your body's way of doing what it has been trained to do. It's natural.

Ⓢ Turn towards 'bad' emotions

This strategy, adapted from *Teaching Clients to Use Mindfulness Skills*, Dunkley & Stanton, is all about learning to face negative emotions (including fear, guilt and shame) head on so that they lose their power and go away much faster. For the sake of simplicity I'm going to use fear as the dominant emotion in this example:

✦ Go somewhere quiet, where you'll be undisturbed, with your notebook and pen. Set a timer for two minutes

✦ Turn your mind to your fear. Either say out loud or write down: 'I'm aware that when I'm fearful...' and try to conjure up the feeling. Does it stem from shame, guilt or another emotion? How does it affect your body? Where in your body do you feel it? How does it make you act or want to act? What does it make you think? Some examples might be: 'I'm aware that when I'm fearful my heart starts racing and my body tenses up. I'm aware that when I'm fearful I start remembering embarrassing moments. I'm aware that when I'm fearful I start feeling angry. I'm aware that when I'm fearful I try to push the feeling away'

✦ After your two minutes are up review how you felt about the exercise. Were you nervous about 'turning towards' a negative emotion? Was it as bad as you thought it would be? Did you feel a bit stupid doing it? Did you learn anything?

This strategy can take a while to get used to. It can be hard to get past the 'I feel like a total plonker' thoughts. However, once you get over that, it's amazing what you can discover about yourself and your mind. Most people who complete this strategy say it wasn't actually as bad as they thought it might be – that you can face a negative feeling without getting swamped by it; that it doesn't have to be all-consuming. You may also discover that one emotion leads to another or is born from another, which will tell you more about your fear. The point of this is to start learning how to recognise your emotions and how they affect you, so that you can stop heading down well-worn negative paths on autopilot.

⑤ Use your body as a warning system

Our bodies reflect our emotions in thousands of different ways. From the more obvious (smiling, grimacing, scowling, gritting our teeth) to the much more subtle micro-expressions that we're not even aware of (flicks of the eye, twitches of the mouth, flaring of the nostrils). These non-verbal cues tell others how we're feeling – but they can also tell us how we're feeling too. Often we don't even realise we're getting Hulk-like furious until we notice our clenched fists. Have you ever caught a glimpse of your reflection and been surprised to see you're scowling or furrowing your brow? Tune into your body more. Pick a time to check in daily, such as whenever you put the kettle on. Make it a new routine. Every time you're waiting for the kettle to boil, ask yourself, 'What is my body saying? Are my shoulders hunched or relaxed? Is my jaw tensed? Are my teeth gritted? Am I picking the skin around my nails?'

This regular daily check-up will act as a warning system for your emotional state, so it won't be such a surprise when you realise you feel fearful, anxious, angry or defensive and you can stop the domino effect of negativity by choosing how you want to react rather than switching to autopilot.

Build up your confidence, self-esteem and compassionate voice

When people with healthy self-esteem do something wrong, or feel attacked, judged or humiliated, they can call on their stores of self-validation to admit their faults or not take things so personally. These stores stop them feeling crushed. Everything you are learning in this book should be bolstering your confidence and self-esteem to the point where you shouldn't need to run away from 'bad' emotions, but can accept them, learn from them and move on. Just the very act of reading this book proves you are willing and able to accept that the way you have been doing things up to now may not be working and you want to make changes. You can cope with difficult situations. You can feel fear and push through it. To do this, you need to build up and listen to your compassionate voice.

⑤ What does your compassionate voice sound like?

We discussed your compassionate voice in Chapter 4 (remember the two wolves battling in your head on page 60?). Think on it again now. When we feel fearful or anxious we can lose our compassion both for ourselves and for other people. To kick-start this way of thinking again, ask yourself 'what does compassion mean to me?' Here are some thoughts:

+ Empathy
+ Kindness
+ Encouragement
+ Wisdom
+ Considerateness
+ Fairness

When you feel frightened, anxious or worried, don't berate yourself or punish yourself for it. Feeling these things is normal. You are not weak to feel them! Listen to your compassionate voice and start showing yourself some empathy, kindness and fairness.

Thoughts to take away

✓ Emotions pass. They are not permanent. Facing your fear will make it pass more quickly

✓ Use shame and guilt as prompts to learn lessons and make changes, not to punish yourself

✓ Engage your compassionate voice when you're being hard on yourself – at least listen to what it has to say!

7

The Second Act

When you're scared of something, you will act in ways that actually aggravate your fears. Realising this and taking steps to behave differently will change how you view your ability to cope. Taking positive action will make you believe that, yes, you CAN handle it.

'Hi. My name is fear. Are you avoiding me?'

When we're scared of something it's our natural inclination to push it away. Pretend it's not there. Stick our fingers in our ears and sing 'lalalalala!' loudly. It's down to those 'bad' emotional flavours described in Chapter 6. We fear our fear and so do everything in our power not to feel it. Avoiding a situation that may frighten us seems to be one of the simplest ways to achieve this aim. But it's not. You're actually just launching yourself into a classic game of 'short-term gain for long-term pain'. You may feel great while you're sinking that gin, watching that cat ride a hoover on YouTube or re-painting your bedroom for the fourth time… but you can't avoid whatever you're frightened of forever. And when it reappears, your fear over it will have grown bigger, like a monster that feeds on rejection. While once you were a little nervous about driving, you're now absolutely petrified. While once you were scared about telling your parents you're gay, you now can't even contemplate the horror of telling them, so insurmountable do the consequences seem.

Avoidance supersizes fear for several reasons:

+ You're not just scared about the 'situation' any more, but also anxious over your avoidance of it
+ You've added guilt and shame over not doing anything into the mix
+ You've spent days/weeks/months making up excuses as to why you can't do it. Facing the issue means facing all of your excuses too
+ Whatever you're putting off may be getting more urgent the longer you leave it, so now you feel rushed and panicky
+ You may feel you've left it too late and so should give up: 'I missed my chance'
+ The longer you avoid something the scarier it seems – you indulge worst-case scenarios, catastrophising and fortune-telling thoughts like, 'This is going to be the most embarrassing thing in the history of the world' – losing all perspective

Most importantly, avoidance doesn't let you see that there isn't actually a threat. You don't ever get to prove to yourself that you actually can deal with whatever it is. Because of this your fear is not only maintained but it grows too. This is why exposing yourself to what scares you or makes you anxious is the cornerstone of CBT. In doing so, you're giving yourself the chance to disprove your fears by seeing that yes, you actually *can* cope with it.

The tap-dancing bear phenomenon

Don't think of a tap-dancing bear. And definitely don't, under any circumstances, think of a tap-dancing bear wearing a waistcoat. Wait – that waistcoat-wearing bear is tap-dancing in your head, right now, isn't he?

When you avoid something you're just ensuring that you can't think about anything else. You're making the subject you fear the focus of your thoughts. Have you ever discussed something with a friend and then ten minutes later heard the same discussion on the news or seen a headline about it in a newspaper? 'How weird is that?' you exclaim. But it's not weird at all. You were focused on that particular thing at the time and so noticed the connections. Avoidance hypes this kind of specified attention because your fear about the subject has designated it a 'threat', so your threat-detectors go into overdrive and try to hunt out anything related to it in order to keep you 'safe'. This is why, if you're trying to avoid your ex, you'll hear their voice everywhere, catch sight of them on every street corner and overhear people talking about them wherever you go. They're not actually on every street corner (unless they're a stalker, in which case call the police pronto), it's just that your body is on edge, ready to scream, 'THERE THEY ARE. RUN AS FAST AS YOUR LITTLE LEGS WILL CARRY YOU' at the slightest sense of danger. It's the same if you're scared of driving. Your attention will latch on to any story that reiterates how dangerous it is. 'Car crash, you say? I knew it!' Your inner critic has an absolutely lovely time ramping up your fear to fever pitch.

The simplest way to stop this madness? Simply start thinking about whatever you're avoiding. Your fear will start to shrink immediately.

Avoidance vs fear

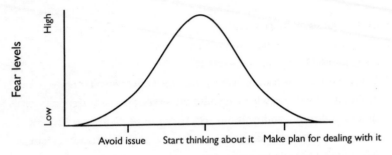

This happens because we feel better about frightening stuff once we know what we're dealing with. At the moment, part of what you fear is the Big Unknown. What will happen? Can I cope with it? Imagine you're white-water rafting and your raft springs a leak, spinning towards a waterfall. Terrifying, right? Now imagine you're hurtling towards the edge, yet you know it's actually not a waterfall at all, but just a small cascade – over which sits a boat-load of cheerful lifeguards waiting to rescue you. All at once, not so scary. It's the difference between seeing a large spider on the wall (fine, I can cope with this – I know it's there) and it suddenly disappearing (OHMYGODWHEREISIT?). Knowing what's happening, or what's likely to happen, makes you feel more in control. Avoiding the situation and pretending it's not happening keeps you stuck on the edge of the waterfall or closing your eyes, praying the spider isn't there.

By starting to think about the issue, your fear will dissipate. You can start working out what's likely to happen and then plan for those outcomes. You make your fear into less of an unknown by facing it.

⑤ How to stop avoiding, and start facing, your fear

There are several stages to this strategy that will demand a fair bit of honesty from you. Addressing these issues will be tough, but stick with it and you'll soon see results.

Stage 1 – Does avoidance work?

1 What situation/issue have you been avoiding?
   Asking my long-term partner to marry me.

2 Using what you've learned throughout this book, why do you want to avoid this situation – what are your mid-level fears (i.e. rejection, disapproval, vulnerability, failure, etc.)?
   Feeling trapped, but also failing at marriage, being rejected, facing disapproval from my wife if I'm not up to scratch as a husband.

3 Despite your avoidance do you still have those fears?
   Yes. If anything I feel a bit worse because I know she's wondering what's wrong, as I'm acting distracted and distant.

4 If your answer is yes (as it will be) can you therefore accept that avoidance on a very basic level isn't working as a strategy for dealing with the issue?
   Yes.

Stage 2 – What does avoidance cost you?

1 How much mental energy do you spend on whatever you're avoiding and also on the guilt over the avoidance itself? Try to measure it in percentile points, e.g. I spend 60 per cent of my mental energy thinking about the situation every day and 40 per cent thinking about everything else in my life.
   I probably spend about 70 per cent of my time thinking about this. Because even when I'm doing something else it's there in the background, whirring away.

2 How has it impacted your health? Do you feel exhausted, run down,

sluggish, tense, nauseous, fidgety, unable to concentrate?

I feel permanently on edge. As if I've left the oven on or something. I can't concentrate.

3 How has it affected your relationships? Are you snappy or short with some people? Do you avoid others? Are you needy, constantly seeking reassurance?

I'm being pretty horrible to my partner. She doesn't know why, of course, and I can't tell her, so I'm taking it out on her for no reason. I'm acting like a pretty awful person, to be honest.

4 Has it affected your self-esteem? Do you question your competence to deal with other situations?

I actually turned down a new project at work because 'I have too much on'. When they asked me what I had on, I couldn't answer! How do I explain it's all just in my head?

Stage 3 – Put in place anti-avoidance strategies

Now you've hopefully accepted that avoidance as a strategy for combating fear not only doesn't work but actually makes things considerably worse, whenever you notice yourself running away from something or pretending it's not happening, follow these steps:

1 Remind yourself of the following:
   + Thoughts AREN'T facts
   + Your thoughts about this subject are twisted up – you can't trust them because…
   + Your inner critic is a jackass
   + Your anxiety about the issue will decrease the moment you decide to face the issue

2 Practise everything you learned in Chapter 3 for stopping fight or flight kicking in. We often associate the emotional flavours we experience (good, bad, neutral) with our physical responses to those emotions, i.e. relaxed and calm, uptight and tense, or neutral. By becoming less frightened of your physical response to fear, you'll become less

frightened of fear itself. (A good way to do this is to think of 'softening' your body. When you tense up your body becomes sharp and angular. Try to make it 'soft' by loosening your muscles.)

3 Remind yourself of how you felt during the 'Turn towards your emotions' strategy in Chapter 6. All emotions pass. They are not permanent. Yes, you may feel frightened, sad or angry, but these feelings will pass. Facing them will make them pass more quickly.

4 Use 'defusion skills'. These defuse your fear by distancing you from your thoughts so you can view them as an observer, seeing them for what they are (streams of words) rather than what they want you to think they are (facts).

   ✦ Visualise your worst-case scenario in a different colour or as a cartoon

   ✦ Label your thoughts: 'These are my fear thoughts, worry thoughts, anxious thoughts, sad thoughts, judgemental thoughts, I'm-not-good-enough thoughts…'

   ✦ Speak these labels aloud whenever you notice a negative thought: 'I am having a fear thought', 'I just had an I'm-not-good-enough thought'

   ✦ When a negative thought pings into your head say, 'Okay, inner critic. I notice you'

   ✦ Picture yourself as a passenger on a train going through a dark tunnel. You can either try to avoid the tunnel by slamming on the handbrake and stopping to scrabble around in the dark looking for an exit (thereby ensuring you actually spend longer in the tunnel) OR you could carry on with your journey knowing you'll reach the end eventually (because the fear will pass)

5 Ask yourself, 'What can I do today that will make tomorrow a better day?' Is your avoidance going to make tomorrow better or worse? Worse, right? So what can you do to make it better? Realising you're setting yourself up for a bad day tomorrow can act as a very effective wake-up call.

6 Say 'I don't' instead of 'I can't'. The phrase 'I can't' suggests an external restriction or a lack of ability on your part – both of which are unfair and most likely untrue. Yet we use 'I can't' all the time without realising the unconscious effect it will have on our mood. For example, 'I can't cook', 'I can't date anyone', 'I can't tell my partner I'm pregnant'. Saying 'I don't' instead may sound weird, but it will make you feel that you've made a choice over the matter and can therefore reverse the decision whenever you want. For example, 'I don't drive', 'I don't date', 'I don't tell my partner news like this'. Re-forming the sentences in this way will make you feel you have more power over the situation: 'I don't drive, *but I could*', 'I don't date *at the moment*', 'I don't tell my partner news like this *until I'm ready*'. Suddenly these aren't things you physically or mentally can't do according to some unwritten rule, but are things you're choosing not to do until you're ready. This small change will make a big difference in how you view your ability to cope with things that scare you.

7 Along the same lines, substitute 'should' and 'must' to 'could'/'can' or 'would'/'will'. 'Should' and 'must' make you feel as though you're following some kind of rulebook that you have to obey, as if you have no choices in whatever you 'have' to do. You always have choices. So instead of, 'I should/must stay in this job I hate', change to 'I could stay in this job I hate… but, then again, I don't have to'.

8 Challenge your fears using the strategies you've already learned. Have you ever dealt with anything like this before? What skills or abilities do you have that suggest you will succeed rather than fail? If things go wrong, wouldn't you feel better for having tried than not having attempted at all? What are the alternative, more positive, views? How might this go right?

The self-sabotage squad

Have you ever been watching a football or tennis match and seen certain players give up? Perhaps they've received a bad call from the referee or have messed up a couple of shots and suddenly they seem to lose the will to compete at all. They shout at themselves or others, deliberately miss shots, watch balls skim past their noses and generally behave as if they couldn't care less. Why? Because they want to fail on their own terms. When things are going wrong, or you anticipate that they might go wrong, deliberately messing them up can feel like a relief because you can tell yourself, 'I failed because I didn't try – not because I'm not good enough. If I had tried my best I would have nailed it.'

Reasons people self-sabotage

+ Wanting to control the outcome of a situation
+ A belief that failure is 'safe'
+ Low self-esteem: believing you don't deserve success or happiness
+ Unrelated self-destructive behaviour influencing the situation, e.g. being drunk or on drugs
+ A desire for drama or excitement through creating conflict or a need to be the centre of attention through gaining sympathy
+ Perfectionism. If it's not perfect, why bother?
+ So that you can be the victim in the situation

Often self-sabotage is prompted by several of the reasons listed above, not just one. For example, imagine you're waiting to hear from your boss about whether you've got a promotion. You can't control your boss's decision, so it's out of your hands. Every day you wind yourself up more and more, becoming increasingly fearful and anxious. When you can't bear it any more and feel you have to regain some control of the outcome, you call up your boss and tell them that, actually, you've changed your mind and you don't want the promotion anyway. You think, 'Phew! Dodged that bullet. It would have ended badly anyway, best not to try.' Or perhaps you're in a great relationship, but start behaving badly by pushing your partner away, staying out late and flirting with other people. Your partner dumps you. You think, 'At least I know why they dumped me. It's not because I'm unlovable or I wasn't good enough – it's because I behaved like an idiot.' (These examples cover at least five of the reasons detailed in the box on page 115.)

In her autobiography *Yes Please*, actor, director and writer Amy Poehler revealed: 'I was never great in auditions. When I was nervous I would often under-prepare and act too cool for school. I would try to reject them before they rejected me, which was confusing since I had decided to audition and acted angry to be there. I remember one particular time I auditioned for the Coen brothers. I realized I was doing a pretty shitty job and I over-compensated by also acting like a dick. The Coen brothers were very nice. I think I have blocked it all out.'

Self-sabotage becomes a self-fulfilling prophecy. You believe you're going to fail so you behave in ways that ensure that you will. For example, Andrew was terrified of being single. He believed that he couldn't cope without his girlfriend. He would constantly ask her, 'You won't ever leave me, will you? You can't leave me. You do love me, don't you?' After six months of this, his girlfriend left him, purely because she couldn't cope with his neediness and constant quest for reassurance. Meanwhile Connie was scared of failing her university course so kept being rude to her lecturer. One day she threw a rolled-up piece of paper at him – and he kicked her off the course. She, of course, blamed him: 'He hated me anyway. I never had a chance.'

Self-sabotage is incredibly damaging because while you think knowing you're going to mess up will in some way limit your disappointment at failing – it doesn't. It actually makes you feel worse as it reconfirms your inner critic's beliefs that you're a bit rubbish. You've also added a bloody great big wedge of guilt and frustration on top for good measure. To stop these emotions piling up, many people resort to telling victim stories in order to justify their behaviour, such as, 'I had no choice', 'It wouldn't have worked out anyway, nothing ever does' or 'They didn't give me enough time', which only serves to aggravate your feelings of helplessness. (Victim stories play such a big role in fear that we've dedicated an entire chapter to them – Chapter 9.)

Acting this way means that you never get the chance to find out whether you could have succeeded, discrediting your fears and shutting up your inner critic's incessant whining.

Ⓢ When did you last trip yourself up?

1 Fill out the trip-up table on page 118 with either the last three times you self-sabotaged or with the three biggest instances of self-sabotage you can remember throughout your life. This will involve digging into some pretty uncomfortable memories and revealing some even more uncomfortable truths. You'll have to get past your victim stories ('I had no choice, so it wasn't self-sabotage') and admit to yourself that you either didn't do something at all or that you did it deliberately badly because you wanted to fail on your own terms.

2 Ask yourself, 'Why did I do that?' To achieve this you're going to have to put yourself back into your shoes at the moment you chose to act in the way you did. What were you scared of? What were your mid-level fears?

3 Next, write down how you felt after you'd self-sabotaged, when the 'event' or situation was over.

4 Finally, note down how looking back on it makes you feel now.

The trip-up table

The act of self-sabotage (include date of event)	Procrastinated and left my dissertation to the very last moment (at university four years ago)	Last week I skipped a party where my friend was intending to introduce me to a woman he thought I'd get on with
Why did you do it? What were you scared of?	I was scared it wouldn't be good enough to get a First… and that I wouldn't get a better grade than my friend, Elle, who I was very competitive with (mid-level fears: disapproval, failure, humiliation)	I couldn't face it – any of it. The thought of starting a new relationship from scratch after my last break-up; the disappointment of not liking her or of her not liking me; the expectation of my eager friends. It made me angry (mid-level fears: rejection, vulnerability, change)
How did you feel afterwards?	Anxious, stressed, tired, but strangely defiant. I told everyone how I'd left my dissertation to the last minute so that a bad grade wouldn't be unexpected and a good grade would make me seem amazing	Resolute. I'd done the right thing. Why should I have to meet anyone? I'm happy on my own. Why does everyone think I need to conform to these social norms, just because they do? In fact, I don't even know why I've included this in self-sabotage – it was self-saviour behaviour!
How do you feel about it now?	Ashamed. I ended up getting a First – and I did beat Elle. But because I'd made such a big deal about how little work I did, I seemed boastful and arrogant. Elle worked really hard and was upset with me – justifiably so – and my result felt a bit grubby. It made me sad to think how well I could have done had I really put the time in – I would have at least felt I deserved the grade I got	My first response to this question was, 'the same', but thinking about it has made me feel a bit crappy. My friends told me the girl was embarrassed I didn't show up, which made me feel bad. I guess I didn't think about her at all – just myself. Maybe I did miss out if she really wanted to meet me. I'm not sure how I feel. I've never thought of myself as a mean person before, so I'm shocked that I might have made someone else feel bad.

Look over your list. Are the situations you wrote down in any way connected, e.g. are they all to do with work, money, how you look, sex, dating or family? What form does your self-sabotage usually take? Do you usually leave things to the last minute, make excuses, blame other people or not try very hard?

Working out these patterns will make you more aware of self-sabotaging tendencies when they come up in the future. Like many of our actions prompted by fear, we can self-sabotage on autopilot, so believing are we of our inner critic's views that we genuinely think we'd be better off skipping something or bodging it up on purpose: 'What if I try my hardest and still fail?' It can also fit into our generalised 'woe is me' worldview: 'What's the point? Nothing ever goes right for me anyway.' Hopefully now you're aware of self-sabotage you'll notice when you're contemplating failing deliberately or not giving something your best shot and can ask yourself, 'Do I really want to do this? How will it make me feel now and in the future?'

Well, that makes perfect sense

Perfectionism is intimately related to shame and fear. We try to be 'perfect' in areas of our life that we're most self-conscious about, that we most fear feeling shame about. It's in the same ball-park as avoidance, self-sabotage and all the other behaviours that we believe protect us against ridicule, judgement, criticism and vulnerability. Perfectionists can't handle the thought of something going wrong. If it does, they'll give up with it all together, berate themselves and everyone else, or put off trying again because unless it's perfect, what's the point?

The motivation behind this, like so much of our behaviour related to fear, is control. Perfectionists think, 'If I'm cleverer, faster, sexier and richer than everyone else, no one can laugh at me, dismiss me or undermine me.' To get to these lofty heights they start seeing the world in a black-and-white way: success or failure, with no middle ground, no grey area. They de-value their achievements and constantly move the goalposts so they can continually beat themselves over the head with a big stick.

Perfectionism is a growing epidemic, fuelled and maintained by the immediacy of social media. We can quantify what makes someone 'successful' by the number of followers or likes their various profiles receive – and, by that very same yardstick, can therefore quantify what makes someone unsuccessful, or a 'failure'. Not only this, but our entire lives are photographed and published online with or without our consent. Even if you don't have a social media account, if you attend an event a photo of you might be posted online by other guests. Your job, appearance and relationships are publicly scrutinised. We can therefore set ourselves unrealistic goals and keep putting ourselves under enormous pressure – which can make us pretty hideous to be around. We can become competitive, dismissive and judgemental of others. We can focus wholly on the one thing in life that's not right, rather than the hordes of other things that are: 'That lamb I cooked should have been pinker. That jog I took should have been faster. That sex I had should have been better' – and, by default, start expecting higher standards from others or belittling their achievements (often totally unconsciously, not realising that an attitude of, 'while this is acceptable to you, it's not to me' is offensive). Living this way makes life a slog. And, if we do manage to one day meet our own near-impossible standards, we'll find something wrong with it, nit-picking at everything until all the fun, spontaneity and joy in life fizzles and dies.

Perfectionism is driven by a fear of what other people think. You need to learn how to think better of others (we're not all judgemental bastards) and also of yourself (you're great as you are – no, really, you are. Perfection is boring, intimidating and alienating).

Ⓢ Do something you'll be rubbish at

Think of something you're genuinely not very good at or that you've never tried before and then sign up to do it. Two left feet? Go swing-dancing. Tone deaf? Join a choir. Don't know the right end of a pencil? It's life-drawing class for you.

Force yourself to face your limitations and embrace them. You can't know everything. You can't be great at everything. And you shouldn't want to be – otherwise you'd never develop and learn. It is our imperfections, mistakes and shared experiences that make us approachable, relatable, likeable and essentially human.

Ⓢ Laugh at yourself

While you swing-dance badly, sing like a seagull or sketch stickmen in life-drawing class, laugh. Laugh long and loudly at yourself. Laughing has so many healing properties, releasing endorphins in the brain, chemicals that activate a natural 'high'. A study by Robin Dunbar of Oxford University found that people who viewed or participated in comedy had higher tolerance towards pain than those who didn't; they could withstand more pain both at the time of laughing and afterwards, showing that laughter has a long-term influence on your mood and body.

If fear is Dracula, laughter is the stake. Physically, your body's response to laughter douses fight or flight, while mentally, finding the humour in a situation means you're actively looking for alternative views to the doom-and-gloom options. It's a choice: 'You have to either laugh or cry, right?' By choosing to laugh, you're being courageous and courage is much more powerful than fear.

Ⓢ Embrace your inner klutz

People like people who aren't perfect. There have been plenty of studies examining the 'pratfall effect' of likeability and they have all confirmed that those of us who stumble, stutter or walk around with our skirts tucked into our knickers are far more likeable than those who never have a hair out of place. Clumsy people are relatable, less intimidating and remind us of ourselves – because none of us are perfect.

S What would your epitaph read?

If it was written today, would it say something like this?:

+ Jane spent time ensuring dinner was perfectly cooked for her guests
+ Emma maintained her perfect size-ten figure for twenty years
+ Tom had the most perfect garden on his street

Is that what you want to be remembered for? Or would you prefer to have something like this?:

+ Jane was incredibly loyal, caring and had the best laugh in the county
+ Emma was fun-loving, kind and made friends wherever she went
+ Tom's generous spirit means that he'll be missed by everyone who knew him

If you were a stranger reading both sets of epitaphs, which set of people would you most like to have known?

Learn how to fail like a pro

You need to redefine how you think about the very word 'failure'. The word itself is emotionally provocative, conjuring up images of people pointing and laughing at you as you prepare to step blindly off a cliff. No one wants to be that guy so you self-sabotage, avoid things or give up after the first knock-back. All of which only perpetuates your belief that you can't cope.

Here's news: failure is a good thing.

Failure leads to success – every time you cock something up, you learn how not to do it, which is an integral lesson on the road to achievement. It's just as Edison said: 'I have not failed. I've just found 10,000 ways that won't work'.

JK Rowling's *Harry Potter* manuscript was rejected by lots of literary agencies before being taken on – as was Stephen King's novel *Carrie*. Walt Disney's first animation company went bankrupt. The Beatles were told by one record label: 'The Beatles have no future in show business'. Oprah Winfrey was fired as a young reporter and told she was 'unfit for TV', and Hillary Clinton lost the 2008 Democratic presidential nomination before coming back to win it (the first woman ever to do so) in 2016.

Imagine if any of those people had given up after their first knock-back. Replace the word 'failure' with 'learning curve', 'lesson' or 'practice', as in, 'Well, that was an interesting lesson' or 'I'm glad I'm being given all these opportunities to practise so I know how to get it right'. It will totally change how you view problems or mistakes.

⑤ Stop thinking of things as 'risks'

Ban the words 'risk' or 'risky' from your vocabulary. They suggest the possibility of danger (usually in the form of failure) which immediately makes you want to find reasons not to do whatever it is you're considering doing. Use the words 'opportunity' or 'chance' instead. So, 'Do I want to take this opportunity?' rather than, 'Do I want to risk this?' This simple change will make you look at the situation more positively.

⑤ Ask yourself, what can I do differently next time?

Learn from what happened. Did you work hard enough? Were you focused? Had you done your research? Is it just a case of wrong place, wrong time? Did you butt heads with someone? Can you try someone or somewhere else? Is there anything you can do differently next time? And, most importantly, do you really believe in what you're doing? If the answer is yes, keep at it. There is always a way in – a side door. Be open-minded about what you can achieve and what you want. Should you go back to the beginning? Are there more things you need to learn? Ask for feedback and advice and listen to that feedback.

Doing something new and putting yourself in the path of failure will always be scary. That's natural. You can't do anything new and not feel apprehensive. It's how you deal with your fear that marks you out.

Thoughts to take away

✓ Avoidance only aggravates fear. Just thinking about facing the issue will make you feel less scared

✓ Self-sabotage is incredibly damaging. Admitting you're tripping yourself up is the first step in feeling brave enough to take more positive action

✓ Perfection doesn't exist and striving for it will limit your experiences and increase your fear. Remember: failure is an invaluable part of achievement

8

Rules of Engagement

We create rules for ourselves to obey without even noticing. Rules that limit our experiences, make us frightened of failure and put us under enormous pressure. It's time to rip up your personal rulebook.

Breaking the rules

Your mind has a list of rules that it expects you to obey no matter what's going on. These rules are based on expectations, judgements and internal standards that your inner critic believes you have to uphold. And, like most stuff your inner critic does, these rules are sneaky by nature – you won't even have noticed you're abiding by them, so entrenched are they in your psyche. This is how it works: your mind makes a two-step plan for dealing with anything – first comes the plan, then come the rules.

The Plan: Do whatever it is you plan to do
The Rules: Abide by a set of rules while you do it that will determine whether you succeed or fail

Janet is about to meet her partner's parents for the first time. That is The Plan: what she has to do. Then, instead of simply going and having a good time, her mind presents her with The Rules – a set of regulations she has to obey while she meets the parents: 'I have to wear something that is stylish, but not too try-hard. I have to compliment them on their house. I have to remember that his dad likes to be called Bob, not Robert. I have to be funny, but not silly. I must only have one glass of wine so I don't get drunk' and on and on. Before Janet's even arrived she's set herself a mountain of tasks to achieve – and if she doesn't achieve them, she'll have failed. Scary, right? Yes. And because she'll be frightened of failing, her anxiety about the meeting will increase. For no reason! These rules have sprung from nowhere and will indelibly alter the evening and eliminate all chance of spontaneity. If Bob (not Robert) asks Janet if she wants another drink, she'll say 'no' even if she does want one. She'll also be aware of making 'silly' jokes, so will hold back on her natural inclination to be light-hearted.

Whenever you follow these rules you limit your own experience. You live in your head, rather than the moment, and damage your self-esteem with self-critical commentary ('You nearly did that wrong', 'I can't believe you stayed later than 10pm!'). By not following her rules Janet could have had three glasses of wine and ended up doing karaoke with Bob after telling some rubbish jokes that made everyone laugh.

We normally accept these rules without question because we believe our mind is on our side, but now you know more about your inner critic hopefully you'll be aware that sometimes it's not. It wants you to be scared, so you stay 'safe'. This means that The Rules are often totally unhelpful and unnecessary. By simply being more aware of them, you'll be giving yourself a choice about whether to listen to them or not. Some of them might be valid. For example, if you're going for a job interview, the rule 'don't hug the interviewer' is probably best obeyed, but 'don't ask stupid questions' can be bent a bit, while 'don't be clumsy' can be outright ignored (we tend to like clumsy people).

Example: Being the best guest

Nathan didn't like attending events where he'd meet new people. He always listened to his fortune-telling thoughts, which informed him he'd have a terrible time. Much of this was connected to the rules he'd lay out for himself before he went out: 'I have to be funny and chatty. I have to ask intuitive questions. I have to remember everyone's names. I have to laugh in the right places and understand the "in" jokes. I can't be dull. I can't let my girlfriend down.' No surprise, then, that he usually did have a terrible time. He put himself under so much pressure he'd spend the whole night on edge. As a result he started withdrawing socially and making excuses as to why he couldn't join his girlfriend at events, which started affecting their relationship.

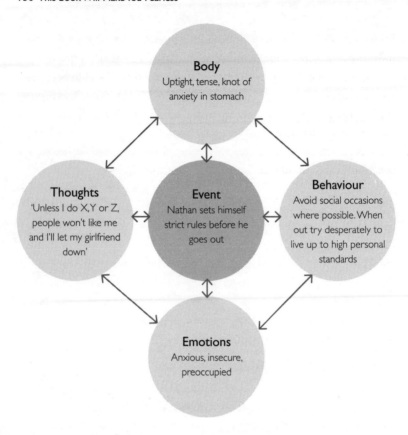

Nathan is so focused on the rules he sets himself that he actually dreads going out. And when he does go out, he's barely present, just trapped in his head. And his rules are ridiculous! You're allowed to be shy and quiet. Lots of people are. No one is funny and chatty all the time. It's natural to forget people's names if you've only just met them and how could you possibly know the 'in' jokes if you're not in on them? The worst thing about it is, his fears actually become self-fulfilling prophecies as whenever he goes out he's paying so much attention to his rules – 'I should say X, but I mustn't say Y' (rules are often characterised by the use of inflammatory words 'should/shouldn't' and 'must/mustn't') – that he doesn't pay any attention to the natural ebbs and flows of the evening. He seems uptight and on edge and he actually does miss the jokes and natural conversational invitations people give him to join in. Nathan blindly follows these rules without questioning them. To him they act as a safety net – 'If I do these things, the night will be a success' – but they limit his experiences and put him under huge unnecessary pressure.

⑤ Become aware of your own rules

Start becoming aware of the rules you set yourself whenever you're undertaking a plan. Notice if your mind presents you with a list of things you have to either do or not do for the event to be considered a success. Things like, 'I shouldn't stay late at Mike's birthday party', 'I mustn't mention Rosie's dad's illness' or 'I can't be too bossy at the pub quiz'.

You'll probably be surprised by how many rules you set yourself – even over totally inconsequential tasks. For example, when you're making a cup of coffee or tea, do you think, 'I must use a good mug' and then carefully select your mug based on a set of preconceived criteria (big and round with a 'proper' handle, I bet)? Are you surprised to realise you have a protocol for mug-choosing?

The rules we set ourselves are based on ingrained notions we've abided by for years and years – often since childhood – so we don't question them, even if they're out of date, out of context or completely farcical. While you can't stop your mind setting these boundaries, by becoming aware of them, you can at least choose whether to abide by them or not, rather than let them ramp up your fear over somehow getting it 'wrong' according to some mythical rulebook.

Other people's rules

Other people have different rules to you. Not just for individual events, but general life rules. Have you ever thought, 'I can't believe they just did that to me! I would never do something like that!' and fumed and raged about the injustice of it? Because we wouldn't do something, we assume the fact that someone else has means it's a personal attack. That they did it on purpose to upset us because they know it's a bad thing to do. Not so. According to their own personal rules, what they've done is probably perfectly acceptable. Left the dishes in the sink for three days? Acceptable. Hooked up with your ex? Acceptable. Applied for the same job as you without telling you? Acceptable. They're not doing it to be horrible; they haven't even realised you may think it is horrible, because, according to their own rules, it's fine.

Realising this can lift a massive weight off your shoulders as you'll stop taking things so personally and will therefore stop being fearful that someone's deliberately out to hurt you or piss you off. They're not. They're just abiding by their own rules. You can then explain gently that some things do upset you or annoy you and go from there without steaming in like a freight train.

The ruminati

The rules you give yourself will be inspired by your beliefs surrounding success and acceptability; beliefs you have grown up with and those you have acquired along the way. These beliefs influence your fears and prejudices and one of the biggest things you can do to confirm these prejudices is to ruminate on past mistakes or regrets.

Ruminating means raking over and over the past, which doesn't help anyone – not you or anyone else featured in your memories. Nit-picking over what you did or didn't do and what you should or shouldn't have done is meaningless in the grand scheme of things if you don't use what you now know to take positive action. Using past behaviour as a predicator of future behaviour is healthy. Use it as a clue as to what you are likely to do again in a similar situation, not as a whip to punish yourself.

Ruminating fosters the feeling that you deserve to feel bad or to fail. You start relishing feeling low and punishing yourself by reliving horrible memories, piling guilt and shame on yourself as you worry about doing the same again (and so set yourself restrictive rules to obey).

Ruminating can also trigger fear snowballs. Imagine you're thinking, 'I can't be bothered to go out tonight', then quickly remember that you cancelled on the same group of people just last week. You start thinking, 'What's wrong with me? Why do I always do this? Why can't I be like Alex, who loves going out?' You now feel fearful about something that has absolutely nothing to do with the situation – going out with your friends. Your fear has snowballed into concerns about your core self. This can lead to making rules to deal with it: 'I must go out and have fun. I must be funny and good company. I must buy all the drinks and look happy to be there.' Brooding shatters your self-esteem and makes you feel as if you can't cope. If you find yourself getting bogged down in distressing memories, try these strategies:

⑤ Do I want to behave that way again?

If you remember behaving a certain way in the past, weigh up the evidence for and against whether it was a positive or negative way to act and use that evidence to decide whether you want to act that way again. How did you feel at the time? How do you feel about it now? What was the result of your actions? How will you use this information in the future?

⑤ Employ all your senses

This is a super-simplified mindfulness exercise that will anchor your focus in the present moment, dragging it back from the past. For anyone who hasn't practised mindfulness before, it will sound a bit bonkers, but give it a go. Ask yourself: what can I see, hear, feel, taste and smell? Then tell yourself what you are experiencing, either out loud or in your head, while breathing in and out regularly.

+ Breathe in
+ I can see the trees waving in the wind outside the window
+ Breathe out
+ I can hear cars driving by on the street outside
+ Breathe in
+ I can feel the cold metal of the pen between my fingers
+ Breathe out
+ I can taste coffee in my mouth from my last sip
+ Breathe in
+ I can smell coffee and a strange rusty scent from the radiators
+ Breathe out

How did you find this exercise? Even if you felt stupid doing it, it will have brought your focus back to the here and now, making you more aware of what was happening both in the world around you and in your own head. Your thoughts will have tried to interrupt: 'What are you doing? Go back to your memories!' but that's normal. Just notice the thoughts as chattering birds in the background and focus back on the present moment.

⑤ Apologise

If you're ruminating over something you feel guilty about and you feel it will help you to come to terms with the event, then apologise. It's never too late to send an email or a letter. You can find a million excuses not to do it ('They'll want to forget about it, they'll be angry I brought it up'), but they may appreciate the effort and at least you'll know you've done all you can. However, it's important not to do this with the aim of receiving some kind of absolution. You have to write the message with the expectation that you won't receive any response at all. You are only doing it because you feel it's the right thing to do. That's it. You can then draw a line under the experience.

⑤ Ask yourself: what good came from it?

This is a really tough strategy. You may have been so torn up with guilt and shame over a past mistake or regret that you haven't even considered that some good came from whatever happened. But it will have; it's the natural result of cause and effect, the ripple in the lake from the thrown pebble. So, think about it openly, honestly and without prejudice: what good came from it?

For example, if you had an affair, force yourself to find some positives:

+ My partner is now with someone much better suited to him/her
+ He/she was forced to stand on their own two feet
+ He/she has told me they feel much more independent now
+ Our kids don't have to live with two miserable parents
+ Our kids like both of our new partners
+ I am happier

Or, if you are a recovering anorexic:

+ My parents seem closer than ever
+ They have made friends with other parents from the clinic
+ I have made some great friends with other sufferers
+ My sister is fiercely independent and has done brilliantly at school because she is so furious with me
+ I've learned that I can cope with difficult emotions and situations

That can't be right because…

In 1957 psychologist Leon Festinger proposed Cognitive Dissonance Theory, which sounds massively complicated, but basically means that we don't like our beliefs to be challenged. We like things to fit neatly with our worldview so that we can reassure ourselves that, yes, we are right about everything and we are correct in behaving in ways that fit with these beliefs (by following our 'rules'). When things not only refuse to fit but actively conflict with our worldview, we experience 'cognitive dissonance' – a fancy way of saying 'we get severely uncomfortable' – and so we look for ways to reduce this dissonance. We do this by actively seeking out evidence that our original belief is correct, by reducing the importance of the conflicting belief or by changing our original belief (which is the hardest thing to do).

Here's an example. Say you're terrified of the prospect of a certain political figure getting into power. You believe he/she is all kinds of terrible. You behave in ways that will ensure they don't get in. You petition against them. Vote against them. Lobby others to do the same. Then you discover that you agree with one of their policies. In fact, it's a great policy and it's one you've been advocating for a long time.

How do you reconcile this new information with your belief that the political figure is 'evil'?

Chances are, you don't. You dismiss the policy – it's actually not that great after all and it won't work. Or you find reasons why the policy isn't that important. 'I actually don't care that much about ecological issues/ immigration/equal pay, etc.' You do this because accepting that your belief – something you've abided by for years – might be wrong is incredibly tough.

What has this got to do with fear? So much! You have believed for years that you can't cope with certain things: rejection, vulnerability, disapproval, change, failure, success, etc. All your deepest fears. Accepting that perhaps this belief in your inability to cope is wrong is going to cause your mind lots of trouble. You'll rebel against it. You'll look for evidence that backs up the belief that you can't cope. You'll search for evidence that backs up your mid-level fears. You'll warp evidence that doesn't fit until it does: 'I only passed the exam because they made it easier this year. I'm still not as good as everyone else.'

You need to accept that your beliefs surrounding your fears aren't true. That how you have been behaving up until now hasn't been working. That the rules you have been setting yourself have only been enhancing your fears and limiting your experiences. To do this is incredibly difficult. Changing beliefs takes time and determination, but hopefully by this stage of the book you're more open to accepting that perhaps you haven't been fair on yourself and that many of your fears are unjustified.

⑤ Stop looking at pictures or reading stories about what you're scared of

Stop fuelling your fear and your anxiety by researching negative stories about it or looking up photos that 'prove' you are right to be scared. It's a form of reassurance-seeking ('See? I am right!'), which actually only makes you more afraid. You are confirming your inner critic's belief that you can't cope and are flawed. STOP.

For one day, pay attention every time you check information (i.e. on the internet, on the radio, on TV or in a book) related to your fear. For example, pictures of celebrities who look 'better' than you or who have 'better' lives. Stories of people who regret a decision they made or who suffered terribly from a mistake. Or friends or strangers who are high-achievers, who you feel inferior to. At the end of the day jot down in your notebook how many times you checked something like this – and be honest – and how you felt at the end of the day.

Over the next few days gradually cut down how often you check. If you checked ten times on day one, check nine times on day two, eight on day three and so on. At the end of every evening jot down how many times you checked and how you felt at the end of the day.

Breaking habits like this takes time, patience and practice. Don't get angry with yourself if you check too many times – just start again the next day. Knowing you're going to have to record the number in your notebook should act as motivation to see the task through.

This exercise is about re-educating your brain. At the moment it believes that checking makes you feel 'safe' and that reassuring yourself that you are 'right' to believe certain things is helpful. This strategy will prove to you that it's not helpful and actually only makes you feel more insecure and fearful. By not feeding your preoccupation, whatever you're scared of will seem less of a 'threat' and you'll feel more in control, stronger and more positive. You'll gradually become more open to finding and believing evidence that conflicts with your previously held beliefs.

⑤ Read stories that conflict with your belief

Actively research stories, articles and social media accounts that conflict with your belief. If you're scared that failing all your exams means you've ruined your life, look up stories about people who had great success despite not being academic. Or how people who had previously failed took additional courses and nailed them. If you're terrified of the prospect of being a single parent, look up blogs by single mums or dads to see how they manage and read papers on the positive experiences for both parent and child.

You need to try to be open-minded in accepting the fact that, yes, you are afraid, but your fear doesn't have to stop you or cause you pain. It's not a sign to RUN AWAY. It's a sign that you're challenging yourself and can push ahead.

⑤ How do you feel today?

Draw a line in your notebook or on a sheet of paper and put it up on your wall. Every morning stick a pin in at the point where you see yourself. Monitor the line – is it moving more to the left or to the right? Knowing which direction you want to go in will inevitably influence the decisions you then go on to make. Moving the pin towards 'fearless' becomes a statement of intent: 'I know I have choices and can make changes'.

Terrified   Fearless

◄───►

Thoughts to take away

✓ Your mind sets you rules to obey whatever you're facing. Recognising this will give you the choice about whether you want to follow them or not

✓ Ruminating crushes self-esteem. Only use past behaviour as a predicator for future behaviour – not as a stick to beat yourself with

✓ When your brain can't reconcile new information with negative beliefs, it dismisses or denigrates that knowledge. Actively try to stop this happening by looking for (and hopefully accepting) conflicting information

9

Own it

Fear can make you feel helpless, as if you have no choices. You can feel a victim of circumstance and blame others (and the world in general) for your situation. This is rubbish! You do have options. You do have choices. You need to take responsibility and start owning your life.

Victim schmictim

Fear comes with its own special victim status: when you let circumstances and/or people dictate what you can or can't do. When this happens, you'll use two ways to describe what's going on, both to yourself and to others:

1 **Victim stories:** You have been forced into doing nothing, maintaining the status quo or acting in certain ways because of circumstances out of your control. 'I have no choice. I did nothing to deserve this. If I take action terrible things will happen.'

2 **Villain stories:** Every victim story has to have a villain, but that villain doesn't have to be a person – it can be the world in general, fate, death, luck or chance. The way you speak about difficult things will be characterised by generalisations, catastrophising and labelling: 'Everything is awful. Phil is such an idiot. It's all his fault. This kind of stuff always happens to me.'

Here's a common example that utilises both: 'I can't do anything. I'm stuck. If I do X, then Y will happen and life will be even worse (victim story). I mean, I've really tried, but I just can't get anywhere. The world is out to get me (villain story).'

Both of these stories make you feel helpless and powerless. You're saying to both yourself and to others that you have no choices. That while other people may be able to make changes, to progress, to be proactive, you can't for oh-so-many reasons. In choosing to believe that you have no choices you are choosing to feel afraid and to stay in your comfort zone (see opposite). Which, even if it's not particularly cosy, glamorous or even satisfactory, at least it's safe, eh?

The thing is – you wouldn't have picked up this book if you were content to stay in your comfort zone. This means you want to stick a toe outside. GOOD. You can. By this stage you should be feeling more confident within yourself, more aware of your inner critic and the fact that

thoughts aren't facts. You'll also be wary of believing worst-case scenarios and of letting negative emotions swamp you (remember: emotions always pass). So, having taken all of that on board, the next step is to start noticing when you play the victim. Shit happens – that's a fact. But it's not the shit that happens which stops you progressing or having a good life, it's the resulting decisions *you* make. It's how you choose to interpret those things and then how you choose to act on them.

Here's an example of two very different ways of interpreting the same situation.

Both Debbie and Kim went through messy divorces four years ago. Debbie slipped immediately into the role of furious, wronged ex. She told everyone who would listen what a bastard her ex was for leaving her, how he'd left her with nothing and she couldn't even afford her mortgage (she hadn't worked for years, relying on his income). She would moan about him to their mutual friends and solicit sympathy from whoever would listen. She'd also drill them for information on him and any positive news would send her into a whirlwind of envy, anger and bitterness. After a couple of years of this, her friends started drifting away – and Debbie used this as 'proof' that single people aren't welcome at social gatherings and that her ex had 'bought' their friendship. When even her kids started avoiding her, she fumed, 'I knew he'd turn them against me!' She told herself (and everyone else) that love was nonsense and so pushed away any potential new relationships – using each false start as 'proof' that she was unlovable. She also started selling her furniture in order to be able to afford to keep the house, because 'I can't get a job. No one will hire someone who hasn't worked for ten years.'

Meanwhile, after grieving for her relationship and taking some time out for herself, Kim realised she would lose her house if she didn't get a job. She hadn't worked for several years either, but had seen a sign for staff at the local gift shop and popped in to ask if they might take her on. They'd already found someone, but recommended another shop nearby that was looking. She went there and explained how she'd previously been a shop assistant in a clothing store, so was good with customers and a whizz at numbers. The owner asked her to come back for a trial the very next day and a year later Kim was assistant manager. The sense of achievement she felt at opening up the shop every day filled her with a pride she hadn't felt for years. Earning her own money gave her a fierce sense of independence that she hadn't even realised she'd been missing, so comfortable had she become with being looked after. She joined a tennis club and also met new people through her work. She started socialising alone; something she'd been terrified of doing. She realised she enjoyed it; enjoyed people asking her opinion on matters without deferring to her quite domineering ex. Her friends and her children found her attitude inspiring.

How you let something affect you is a choice. Are you going to be the victim – passive and helpless in the face of misfortune or mistreatment – or are you going to do something about it? It doesn't matter what's happened to you or how awful it was, choosing negativity and helplessness will always produce negative and helpless results, while choosing positivity and proactivity will always produce positive and powerful results. Yes, even if you fail or make mistakes along the way, it'll still be positive because at least you're owning them. At least they're your mistakes and failures. At least you're grabbing life by the scruff of the neck rather than just waiting for someone else to come and save you. No one can change you; you have to choose to change yourself.

The benefits of 'I can't'

If the things written so far in this chapter strike an uncomfortable chord deep down, in the bits of your mind you don't like to examine too deeply, then wait for it – it's about to get a lot more uncomfortable. Ask yourself this: 'What do I get out of being the victim?' You say, 'Nothing! Nothing at all! It's awful! I'm trapped and frustrated. If things were different I'd be living an extraordinary life!' But really? Would you?

I'm going to ask you to complete a strategy now that you will hate. Your entire being will rebel against it. Your inner critic will refuse to engage with it. But you have to do it. If you truly want to feel fearless, this is one of the biggest hurdles to overcome.

Ⓢ Your 'I can't' benefits table

1 In the bottom row of the table on page 146, find positives for each example situation included. It doesn't matter if the examples do or don't relate to your own experiences – answer them as if they're part of an exam or as if they were happening to a friend. I have filled out one full example to help you out.

How did you find this exercise? Looking for positives in other people's situations is always easier than in your own because we have a tendency to believe that what we are experiencing is infinitely worse than what anyone else is going through: 'You wouldn't understand', 'No, that's not the same at all'. Sound familiar? We can get so wrapped up in our own pain, we think no one has ever gone through anything similar and so can't relate to

The 'I can't' benefits table

Situation	Ed is 'trapped' in an unfulfilling job. He can't leave because he has a mortgage to pay and a family who rely on him. Also, the job market is terrible – he'd never find another job anyway	Alice can't leave her relationship. She wants kids and at 37 it's too late to meet someone else and start all over again	Caroline will never go travelling. She missed her chance and now she's got a great career she can't leave and a partner who doesn't want to go travelling at all
Why it's awful (the cons)	He's frustrated and bored	She and her partner have nothing in common. They've grown out of each other and she doesn't want to have sex with him any more	It's something she's always wanted to do – it's sad she'll never fulfil that ambition
Why it might be good (the pros)	It's safe. He's lucky to have a job and a payslip. It's also easy. He doesn't have to try too hard. At least he doesn't hate the job; it's bearable	Write the pros for Alice's situation here:	Write the pros for Caroline's situation here:

it. Even if someone has been through the *exact same* thing, we'll dismiss it as 'different' somehow. They must have been stronger than us to cope with it or they had a better support system than we did. Sometimes it takes an outsider to flag up how silly this is and that it simply isn't true.

2 Add another column to the table above. This one is for the situation you yourself are facing. What do you feel frightened, frustrated or angry about? Why is the situation so awful? And then, finally, why might the

situation be beneficial to you? For example, if you're scared of flying, the cons are obvious – but so are the benefits, no? You get to control where you go on holiday. You get to control where you go on work trips. You get to feel 'safe' within a community and country that you know. You don't have to test yourself by stepping outside your comfort zone. Or, if you're scared of telling your family you're gay, consider this: isn't it easier to keep everything the same? To not rock the boat? To not deal with the ramifications of your family knowing? To not have to bother dealing with their feelings about it? To keep your life secret from them – it is your life after all, isn't it?

It's uncomfortable to realise that there are benefits to not taking responsibility for your fear. That there might be other things motivating you to stay where things are safe. That it might not be the work of outside forces. But acknowledging these pay-offs can make you feel less guilty. For example, in recognising that she feels safer in a relationship, no matter how unsatisfying that relationship is, Alice will feel less guilty towards her partner – she is, after all, getting something out of the union. This will make her feel more in control of her own situation.

The blame game

In the examples illustrated in the 'I can't' benefits table, Ed was blaming his family and the crappy job market for his situation – they were the 'villains'. Alice was blaming her partner and her body clock for working against her. Caroline was blaming her job and partner. All of this blame was unconscious. If you asked Ed, 'Do you blame your family for this?' he would have been aghast, as would Alice and Caroline. But that's exactly what they're doing. And the blame can be totally overt too: 'It's my dad's fault I have to look after him. If he hadn't smoked for half his life, he wouldn't be ill now' or 'It's my son's fault I can't trust him'. In the column you filled out with your own situation, who or what are you blaming? Your boss, son, daughter, wife, husband, niece, nephew, parents, government, society at large? Write down clearly in your notebook what or who you blame.

Taking responsibility

When you were writing down who you blamed, did you think, 'Yeah, but it really is their fault!'? That's totally understandable, but it's also totally wrong. YOU create your thoughts and your actions. No one else. How you choose to deal with your son is your choice. Not his. The fact that you've chosen not to get a new job is your choice, not the economy's. Until you can accept this, you will always feel stymied by other people and by circumstance. You have to start taking responsibility for your life.

Look back over Ed's situation in the 'I can't' benefits table. Imagine he asked you, 'But what can I do about it?' What would you tell him? Perhaps something along these lines:

+ Lots of other people are finding jobs despite the bad market conditions
+ Have you even looked for another job?
+ If you're stuck in your job have you considered trying to make it more interesting?
+ Have you made any moves at all within your own company?
+ Instead of just complaining, have you offered any solutions to improve what you don't like at work?

Ed's gut response would no doubt be, 'Yeah, that's all well and good, but…' and he'd reel off excuses about why he can't do any of those things. He can. He's just refusing to own his life, to take responsibility for it. It's the same with Alice. If you said, 'It's not too late to meet someone else. Plus lots of women have children in their 40s with or without a partner' her gut-reaction would be to find reasons why her situation is different or to point out the difficulties in what you say. But no one can make you happy. If you expect anyone else – or anything else – to make you happy, you are not taking responsibility for your own happiness. This doesn't mean that taking action is going to be easy, but it does mean you acknowledge that you can take action.

⑤ Interrogate your situation

Apply what you just did for Ed to your own situation. Ask, 'If I had to take responsibility for this, what might I do differently?' For example, if you don't trust your son not to drink too much when he goes out, ask yourself: 'Do I have reason not to trust him? Is his behaviour not similar to mine at his age? Why do I feel I still need to protect him? Can't he make his own way and make his own mistakes? Can't I let him find out who he wants to be through trial and error? Isn't that what growing up is all about? Might I be scared of his growing up? Might I be worried he doesn't need me any more? Could I deal with his anger in a different way?'

Taking responsibility doesn't mean blaming yourself

Realising that you have to take responsibility for how you react to everything that happens to you is a huge deal. And it can make you feel like crap: 'All of this is my fault?' No! You have to remember that you have always done what you thought was right at that particular time, knowing what you knew then. Don't ruminate on the past or agonise over the future. Just use what you now know to handle things differently. Blame – of others, or yourself – gets you nowhere.

Learning how to identify when you are not taking responsibility

There are lots of clues you can look out for to spot when you might be slipping back into a victim mentality:

+ Feeling envious or jealous
+ Feeling helpless
+ Ruminating on the past
+ Wallowing in disappointment
+ Being impatient with others and yourself
+ Blaming others
+ Attempting to control others
+ Putting others down
+ Not accepting your own mistakes
+ Never apologising
+ Indulging in perfectionism
+ Becoming addicted to drink, drugs or work

Example: Lauren's late rage

Lauren's friend David was always late. And he never apologised. It was just 'his thing'. It had been this way for years, yet it was getting worse. Where once he'd be 20 minutes late, now he'd rock up an hour late and think nothing of it. Lauren was getting more and more furious the longer she waited. Her heart would start pounding and her hands would shake. 'He doesn't respect me! He thinks his time is more valuable than mine!' Yet she didn't say anything. She didn't sit him down and have a civilised chat about it – she would just be cold towards him when he turned up.

Lauren was blaming David for her rage. Fair, right? He was the one who was always late, after all. But who did her rage really affect? Just Lauren. Her rage wouldn't change David's habits of a lifetime. Lauren had to take responsibility for how she felt. So she did. She asked herself what she was getting out of it – what positives were there in her anger? And she found one – a pretty grim

⋯⋰

⋯⊹

truth. Her fury made her feel superior. The fact that she could look angry and tap her watch and make David feel bad made her feel good in a deep, dark part of herself that she didn't like very much. Acknowledging that was a big deal. Did she really want to be that person? No.

She mentioned to him, calmly, that she was really busy at the moment so if he could try to turn up on time she'd appreciate it. She also started taking a book with her whenever she planned to meet him so she could read it while she waited – she didn't feel the time was such a waste. She decided she'd enjoy it instead. She owned her reaction and choose not to let it drive her to distraction. And because she had made that decision, it didn't.

Taking responsibility can make you realise some pretty awful things – one of which will probably be that some of your decisions may have been quite selfish along the way. Like Lauren, whose anger was motivated by a desire to punish David, and also Alice, who hadn't considered her partner's feelings at all in her frustration at being 'trapped' by him. Because she believed she was in some way 'better' than him, she assumed she was doing him a favour in staying, but it doesn't sound like much of a favour to anyone outside the relationship. We can be so busy martyring ourselves we don't realise we're actually stepping on other people or dismissing their ability to cope with difficult situations themselves.

Owning your life will make you feel powerful and strong. It will make you believe you can step out of your comfort zone because no matter what happens to you, you are in control of your reactions. Knowing this will make your world look like this instead:

You need to CHOOSE

Every single moment of every single day you choose how you are going to feel. You choose how you are going to act. Everything is a choice. You can't control what will happen to you on any given day when you step out of the door, but you can control what you choose to do about it. Life isn't all about the results, it's about the journey and you have to choose how you want to experience that journey.

Are you going to torture yourself over your dad's death and hate the world or are you going to celebrate his life and look forward to using what he has taught you in your own future?

Are you going to blame your partner for holding you back and forcing you to settle or are you going to make changes and feel empowered?

Are you going to dread seeing your family and put yourself down for not standing up for yourself or are you going to take things less personally and stand up for yourself?

Are you going to stay in a dead-end job you hate or are you going to get another job?

Are you going to **choose** misery or fulfilment?
Are you going to **choose** frustration or proactivity?
Are you going to **choose** judgement or inclusivity?
Are you going to **choose** disappointment or motivation?
Are you going to **choose** envy or inspiration?
Are you going to **choose** fear or courage?

You have control over your life. You are not a victim of circumstance. You can own your circumstances. Accepting that you have choices will make you fearless.

Thoughts to take away

✓ Start recognising when you're telling victim stories and ask yourself, 'Do I want to be a victim?'

✓ Acknowledging what you're getting out of your fear (the benefits) is a big step in recognising that you have power over what's happening to you

✓ Everything is a choice. You choose either fear or courage. Choose courage!

10

Life of Pie

Having a full and varied life will make you feel stronger, braver and less vulnerable and fearful. This chapter will teach you how to find meaning where it matters in your life.

Your life as slices of pie

Imagine that this pie chart represents all the different aspects of your life. It is perfectly balanced, each section taking up as much time and attention as the other sections.

Yes, it's neat and tidy, but it's also massively unrealistic. Most of our life pies look more like this, with one section dominating everything else.

Some of the sections even disappear completely. Community? Who has time to do anything in the community? Not me. Personal growth? You must be joking. I don't even know what that means. Well, it's time to learn because here's a fact: people who live well-rounded lives are much happier and more fulfilled. They are more fearless. People whose life pies look more like the first one tend to enjoy life more, have a more positive outlook and deal with fear in much more helpful ways.

No, I'm not ordering you to drop everything and start building an orphanage, but rather suggesting that you consider your own life pie, see where things may be lacking and start taking steps to even up the slices a bit. Why? Because if your life pie is 75 per cent work and then you lose your job, you'll be left staring into a terrifying great black hole and your chances of feeling fearful will be far, far greater.

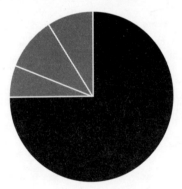

It's the same if the giant section is 'family' or 'partner'. If you spend 90 per cent of your life focused completely on your relationship or family and then go through a divorce, suffer a bereavement or your kids grow up and leave home, 90 per cent of your life simply disappears. It's enough to make even the strongest person feel adrift, rudderless and very, very frightened. While it will be hard to maintain an equal balance at all times, it is essential to try to find some balance. That way, when things shift and shudder in one section – as they will, that's life – you have other things to fall back on.

Examples of black-hole pies

Ava's job was her whole life. She worked every hour she could. She loved her role as client manager in a big advertising firm and would volunteer to take clients out in the evenings and over weekends. Her friendships gradually faded away as she rose up the ranks, but she didn't care. Her job gave her life meaning and was the source of all her confidence and self-esteem. And then she was made redundant. As one of the highest earners in the firm, she was the first to go. It was a staggering blow. The rug had been pulled from beneath her. She didn't know where to turn. Her greatest fear had come to pass.

Christina had dedicated her entire life to her kids. She'd given up her job and raised them while her husband worked (making sure they all knew what she'd sacrificed in order to do this). She was head of the PTA, ran a mums' coffee morning and made sure she was involved in every aspect of the children's lives. Then they left for university and Christina's house was empty. She felt bereft and strangely resentful. Except her house wasn't empty – her husband was still in it. But he didn't count. She'd lost touch with him a long time ago, only relating to him in terms of their kids.

James was a running nut. He lived for the weekends, when he would pull on his trainers and join his running group for 20-mile jaunts in the countryside. He didn't care about his job, just working for enough money to upgrade his gear and pay for his running trips abroad. His only friends were in this running group. He even skipped his brother's stag do because it clashed with a run meet. One Saturday he lost his footing on some uneven ground, fell down a river bank and broke his leg. He couldn't run for three months. He sat at home with his leg in plaster staring at his phone, feeling the lowest he'd ever felt. What now?

Ava, Christina and James each made one thing 'their whole lives'. When those things weren't available any more for various reasons they felt an intense panicky loss, a kind of neediness. They lost the meaning in their lives – what they lived for. Be aware of creating meaning in only one section of your life. And be especially aware if that section is reliant on somebody else. It's not fair on them or you to plonk your entire reason for living on their shoulders. This can come from a misguided sense of being 'good' – a 'good' mother, father, daughter, son, wife or husband. It's not 'good'. It's detrimental to everyone – especially to you.

⑤ Your life pie

Draw a circle in your notebook and list these eight categories underneath it: family, friends, partner/dating, work, community, personal growth, hobbies and alone time. A clarification on some of these:

+ Personal growth: anything to do with the wellbeing of your mind, body and soul, such as religion, spirituality, meditation, therapy or mindfulness (reading this book counts!)
+ Community: work for the good of other people (e.g. volunteering)
+ Hobbies: activities you undertake in your downtime that give you pleasure
+ Alone time: enjoying your own company, feeling happy by yourself

Now divvy up the circle into rough percentage 'slices' representative of how much life you spend on each one (bearing in mind the perfect balance would be 12.5 per cent each). Assess this by considering the literal amount of time you spend doing each and also the headspace you give each – how much you think about it. And be honest.

Are there any slices that are majorly out of proportion? Are there any slices that don't exist at all? Looking at your pie like this, are you shocked by how much of your life is taken up by one thing? Or are you perhaps more shocked at the suggestion that perhaps it shouldn't be? Just to remind you: aiming for 12.5 per cent each is unrealistic, but you should be aiming to find *some* balance, to even things up a smidge.

Making a new life pie is a tough ask. It's re-assessing how you've chosen to live your life. It will take time, patience and practice. But it'll be worth it. Logic dictates that having more variety in your life will lead to a fuller life. It's just common sense. It wards against loneliness, neediness and depression. Sure, if you haven't worked for years, the 'work' section will be empty and maybe you want it to stay that way. But think about it – having daily tasks that make you feel useful will give your life meaning. If these tasks are split between your partner, kids *and* work, you'll be busier. If you can't get a job at the moment, for whatever reason, maybe you could tie work into volunteering – work's not all about making money. It's about feeling useful. Walking someone's dog for them if they're indisposed is useful. Shelving books in the library is useful. Spending an evening reading to an elderly person is wonderful!

Think on that 'community' section a little more. You may feel you have no time for charity work, but being generous with your time for no other reason than to help someone else (not to bolster your own ego) is one of the most satisfying things we humans can do. A brain-scan study by the University of Oregon found that just considering being charitable activated the brain's pleasure centres and several other studies that focused on the lifespan of elderly volunteers have suggested that altruism can actually prolong your life! It's a fact: giving decreases stress and promotes cooperation, empathy and social connection.

Expanding your life to include more time for other things, people and yourself is possible to do and will make you feel happier, more content and therefore much more fearless about facing new challenges.

S How to create a more evenly sliced life pie

1 Put a page aside in your notebook for each of the eight sections. Underneath each heading consider what you could do to make that section more fulfilling. Here are a few ideas:

  + Ensure that I see my friends at least once a month. Book them in early. If I can't see them, schedule a phone call
  + Send my friend who I haven't seen for years a message asking how they are
  + When I'm with my kids focus wholly on them, putting my phone away
  + Book in half an hour each evening before bed just for me. Tell everyone this is 'me time' and I'm not to be disturbed. Make it a routine. Then read a book, have a bath or listen to some music
  + Sign up to the community website and contribute local restaurant reviews
  + Actually drop those clothes off at the charity shop rather than driving them around in the boot of my car for another eight months
  + Volunteer to do a careers talk at my old school
  + Actually book that refresher tennis lesson I've been talking about
  + Leave work on time at least two days this week
  + Ask my neighbour if he needs me to get his shopping for him after his eye op

Change isn't going to happen immediately; this will be a gradual process, but there is one thing to bear in mind that will help hugely…

2 Commit 100 per cent to whatever it is you are doing at the time. When you are with your friends, commit to being with your friends. When you are at work, commit 100 per cent to being at work. Susan Jeffers, in her iconic book *Feel the Fear and Do It Anyway*, has a great way for thinking about this: 'act as if you really count'. She uses the example of a woman working in a temporary job who felt she couldn't commit because the

job didn't mean anything to her. Jeffers asked what she would be doing in that role 'if she really counted'. The woman answered that she'd probably create daily goals, a pleasurable work environment and interact with other staff members in a positive way. Jeffers advised her to do that for a week – and the results were dramatic. The woman reported how she'd brought in a photograph and plant to put on her desk, made sure she completed all her tasks well and on time and made a point of chatting to other people in a positive, friendly way. Investing herself in this way – acting as if she really counted – increased her self-esteem and energy levels and it rubbed off on everyone around her. She mattered and she made a difference.

3 Remember, just because something might not last forever doesn't mean it can't be meaningful. For example, a temporary job, a rented home or a substitute role in a sports team. You can make all of these your own. Choosing to commit fully to every section of your pie will eliminate boredom while increasing interest and confidence.

4 Make a list of goals you want to achieve for each section. Nothing is too big or too small. Things you've always wanted to try. Break the big ones down into smaller, more achievable steps. For example, instead of 'learn to scuba dive', write 'Step 1: Look into scuba classes', 'Step 2: Sign up to class', etc. This will make each thing seem less intimidating, more realistic and will motivate you to see it through as you tick off the stages. Any time you hit an obstacle find ways to work around it, e.g. if you can't afford the scuba class ask the school if there's a payment plan or your partner for a loan or simply wait, save up and sign up for the next round of classes. Whatever you do, don't give up. There's always a way in.

5 Don't be guilt-tripped into stopping by others. The people who you used to dedicate 90 per cent of your time to may well resent your new, busier life. This is a natural response to someone who is withdrawing attention. However, once people see how much happier and confident

you are, they should realise that it's good for you and they will be happy for you. If they're not, you need to manage their expectations and explain that this is a change that is here to stay. If they're still not happy for you, perhaps you need to re-think their place in your life, distancing yourself for a while, but staying strong within your own convictions. (This obviously doesn't count with young kids who may miss having mum or dad there full-time, but they will come to appreciate the new energised you.)

Visualise your life as you want it

Visualisation can take a bit of getting used to, but it absolutely works. It's something actors and athletes have done for decades to get them in the right mindset for upcoming performances and competitions. Essentially, you imagine yourself succeeding: the best-case scenario. In visualising how you achieve something, you convince your sceptical brain (your inner critic) that it's possible. We always believe our negative imaginings of things going wrong, yet we rarely picture ourselves winning. And, with any visualisations vivid enough, you experience the emotion you would if the event actually played out that way. So, if you imagine yourself looking like a complete prat in front of people, you'll feel anxious and humiliated and probably even experience the physical effects: your stomach dipping and your cheeks turning brick-red. The same goes for positive visualisations. If you picture something brilliant happening, you'll experience feelings of pride, happiness and courage. This will motivate you to make it happen – to work around obstacles and to push through fear to see it through, because you've already seen it's possible in your head. Makes sense, right? So give it a go. Here is a simple visualisation technique that focuses on one example. (This strategy involves closing your eyes. It may be worth reading all the instructions through until you can remember it by heart or try recording it onto a device so that you can play it back while you are sitting.)

⑤ Your good-time visuals

1 Go to a quiet place, where you won't be disturbed for at least 20 minutes. Turn off your phone. Sit or lie down. If you're sitting, make sure your feet are flat on the floor. Close your eyes.

2 Think of one of the goals you've written down that you would like to achieve. Let's say it's 'living on my own'. Picture yourself standing in front of the door to your new flat. What can you see, hear, smell or feel? Let your imagination flow. What is the door like – wooden, plastic, painted? Can you smell the flowers near the doorstep?

3 Put the key into the lock and push open the door. You enter a warm room. What colour are the walls? Are there any pictures hanging up? Is there lots of light? Is there a fire in the living room? Walk around your flat. Is there carpet or wood flooring? What sound do your feet make as you walk? Run your hands over the furniture. Take deep breaths in each room as you walk through.

4 Appreciate the fact that everything in this flat is yours and yours alone. No flatmates are lying on the sofas with their music blaring from the stereo or the crap telly show they love playing in the background. It's all yours. Exactly as you want it.

5 Sit down on the sofa in your living room and turn your attention to yourself. What are you wearing? What's your body language saying? How do you feel? Relieved, calm, tranquil, excited, happy, peaceful, inspired? Stay a moment with that feeling.

6 Open your eyes.

The more detailed and intricate you make the visualisation the realer the image will become and the less likely it is that annoying critical thoughts are going to be able to butt in. It's a great process of strategising too. By visualising how you get from Point A to Point B you can plan what you're going to do and how you're going to do it. Then, by remembering the feeling you experienced as you succeeded you'll be motivated to see the goal through. You can call up the image and the feeling whenever you hit a problem and remind yourself why you're working towards it. (You can use this technique for problems too, not just goals. For example, visualising yourself standing up to a bullying colleague and seeing the conversation going calmly and well.)

Your social network

Don't live alone inside your fear. Social support is an integral part of feeling brave. Fear can make us feel incredibly lonely and realising you are not alone can make all the difference. Whatever you're going through and whatever you've experienced: you are not alone. Social support is the biggest barrier we have against fear, anxiety and depression. Knowing that people care and that you are connected makes you feel courageous and able to cope with whatever you're facing.

Ⓢ Find support groups

There are people out there in the world who have been through similar stuff and didn't only survive, but thrived. They're no different to you. They don't have super-powers you don't. They simply chose to thrive, chose to interpret what happened to them as something they could cope with. You can do that too. Speak to those people. Find them. There are grief groups, eating-disorder groups, divorce groups, single-parent groups, depression groups – all full of people who want to grab life by the balls.

Ⓢ Say yes to invitations and invite people out yourself

See your family and friends. You have a ready-made support network right there. Say yes to invitations and issue invitations yourself. Don't isolate yourself. Remember: how you feel before you go out ('I can't be bothered') will have no bearing on how you feel when you're out ('I'm actually having a laugh'). Sure, it's easier to sit on the sofa in your pants, but you're missing a golden opportunity to feel better. You don't even have to talk about what's going on or how you feel – just be around other people. It'll make you feel lighter. And then, when it comes to it, you'll be in a better position to be able to tell people what's going on – if you want to.

❺ Fade out the mood drains

Beware of people who bring you down. We all love a moan occasionally, but there are certain people who get off on it. They try to find common ground with others through gripes and bitchiness, not shared experiences and positivity. These people are mood drains. You start the evening feeling upbeat and positive and finish feeling as though you've been punched by the sad-face emoji.

You can continue hanging out with people who you know bring you down through a sense of obligation, if perhaps they're old friends or have helped you out occasionally. Don't. Things change and people change – and you, hopefully, are changing. You don't owe anyone friendship. Constantly talking about things that make you angry, sad, jealous or bitter will, surprise surprise, only make you feel angry, sad, jealous or bitter. On this road to fearlessness you've hopefully realised that casual words, thoughts and actions have a huge influence on how you feel emotionally. Constantly moaning will make you feel low. It's a fact. If you're serious about feeling stronger, stop moaning – and stop hanging out with people who just moan. Instead, take positive action. If something is wrong, make moves to change it. Don't be passive.

Once you're aware of people who make you feel low, stop indulging their moans. When they start ranting and raving, change the subject or look for the positives, for the alternative views. Verbally challenge their inner critic. Once your friend realises you're not enabling their attitude they'll either change tack or drift away. If they change tack and also start looking for the positives, that's great, but if they don't, let them go. People who constantly share their negative views want to be told, 'Yes, that is awful. You were wronged. Other people are much luckier than you.' If you stop telling them this, they'll look for reassurance elsewhere. Let them. It'll be hard, but worth it for your peace of mind. Life's too short.

⑤ Move on from past hurts

We can hold on to grudges, resentments and anger through a sense of injustice, when we feel someone doesn't understand how much they've hurt us and haven't properly atoned for it. But who wins there? No one. Certainly not you. Holding on to past hurts feeds our fears for the future. It makes us feel like victims and makes us feel helpless.

I'm going to ask you to try something that will sound ridiculous, but do it anyway. Please think about a past hurt that you're still holding on to and say, out loud, 'I'm going to move on'. Go on, humour me. Say it. How do you feel? Stupid, probably, but also a little better? A little stronger? A little less angry? Say it again with more conviction this time: 'I am going to move on'. Say it, even if you don't mean it in the slightest. Just do it. Now how do you feel?

Saying this out loud will make you feel better because you're asserting that you are going to take control of your feelings. Rather than letting anger or bitterness cloud your mind (both of which are hiding your fear over what happened and what it means), you're owning the feeling and taking control: 'I am letting this go'. These are proactive statements that speak of power. They are not helpless or vulnerable in the slightest.

Now, to truly try to mean what you say, go back to a previous strategy. Ask yourself, 'What good came out of it?' and force yourself to find some positives in whatever happened. For example, if someone robbed you and stole all of the jewellery you inherited from your grandmother, what good came out of it? 'I realised I didn't need her jewellery to remember her by. I think about her every day. Her memory is stronger than I knew. It was good that no one was hurt. The police got a lead on the burglars and caught one of them so that guy can't do it to someone else. It also made us realise that material things don't represent people.'

Good things do result from truly terrible events and acknowledging this will make it easier to move on. I read an interview recently of a mother whose daughter was killed in an accident. The interviewer asked her how she managed to cope and the mother spoke of her passionate commitment to the charity she'd set up in her daughter's name and all the brilliant work it was doing. She also spoke of the other grieving parents she'd met who had offered their support and how, through the worst possible thing that she could ever have imagined happening to her, she had experienced a kindness and compassion in strangers she had never believed possible.

You can choose how you let events affect you. Moving on does not mean forgetting, but it will alleviate the pain, helplessness and powerlessness you feel over whatever happened.

⑤ Ask for help

Asking for help is not a weakness, it's a strength. No one can be expected to know everything or be strong 24/7. Feeling fear and anxiety sometimes is totally and utterly normal. Ask for help. Don't just blunder on feeling like crap. Just the act of asking will make you feel better. And if someone rebuffs you, ask someone else. Asking is a brave thing to do in itself. It is proactive and will make you feel less vulnerable and powerless. Whatever form the help takes – advice, taking on more chores, handling some of your workload, looking after the kids for an evening – you'll feel more in control for having asked. Everyone needs help sometimes and we respect those who ask, rather than those who pretend everything is fine while getting increasingly frazzled. And people love being asked for their help. It makes them feel proud that you value their advice, expertise or time. How do you feel when someone asks you for help – honoured, trusted and respected, right?

Your new bravery mantras

You may scoff at 'feel-good quotes' because most of them are complete guff. Stuff like, 'Two inches of snow never stopped the leopard staring you in the eyes'. But genuine affirmations that make you feel motivated and that speak to what you're going through can be truly motivational. Here are some that might help you when you're feeling scared. Write them down in your notebook and read over them whenever you feel the first stirrings of fear:

I *can* cope

I *will* handle it

I am not alone

I am not a victim

I have choices

Other people have got through this, survived and thrived

I am a strong person

I am a worthy person

Thoughts to take away

✓ Having a full and varied life will make you happier, more content and more fearless

✓ Visualising what you want is a brilliant way of strategising and building confidence

✓ Building a network of supportive people will make you feel stronger and brave enough to face any challenge

A final message

Yes! You've made it to this final message! That deserves some triumphal music played across a ticker-tape parade. In the absence of any of that, though, please high-five yourself and have a well-earned glass of fizz. Hopefully you feel much more fearless now than when you first picked up this book. Just the fact that you've taken action and chosen not to let fear and anxiety inhibit your life any more is something to be massively proud of. Many people continue through life feeling unsatisfied, unfulfilled, trapped, worried and frightened. They are scared of making changes, of stepping out of their comfort zone, of not feeling 'safe'. Hopefully reading this book and practising the strategies has made you realise that fear isn't something to be frightened of, it's a natural part of life. Accepting it and respecting are the first steps in learning how to push through it and achieve what you want to achieve. Facing up to how fear affects you personally and deciding you want to make changes will have been seriously tough, so don't underestimate the courage it has taken to get to this stage.

As a means of reflecting on what you've learned so far, please answer the following questions:

1 **After reading this book how do you feel?**
   A The same
   B Interested. Starting to consider what it all means
   C Better. I'm making changes
   D Brilliant. This book has transformed how I think about my ability to cope

If you answered a) can you say you honestly invested time and energy on the strategies? Did you try them all? Did you dismiss some chapters?

Did you come at this with an open mind? Did you think, 'None of this relates to me – my situation is different?' If so, are you willing to try again? To consider the fact that you do have choices and options? Ask yourself: do I want to change things? Is it in my power to do so? If you still feel it's not, please speak to your doctor who may be able to suggest further treatment. If you answered b) – d) then congrats! That is wonderful news. Just starting to consider doing things differently and thinking about things differently is the hardest part. You're well on your way to feeling better.

2 **Are you willing to accept that fear is a natural part of life and not something to be 'fixed', avoided or dreaded?**

This is a major step in feeling fearless – accepting fear for what it is and not being frightened of it. You will always feel scared when you're doing something new or stepping out of your comfort zone. This isn't a sign to retreat or to stop, it's a sign that you're challenging yourself and pushing your boundaries, which is only a good thing.

3 **Are you going to be more aware of your inner critic and not believe everything it says?**

Your inner critic is a mean, miserable bastard, speaking to your worst fears about yourself. Don't trust what it says. You've believed it for a long time so challenging it will be tough, but it's so important. Weigh up the evidence for and against its rants and then make your decision on how to react. Be fair on yourself.

4 **Are you going to nurture your compassionate voice?**

Yep, it sounds cheesy, but it works. Beware of how you speak to yourself, the words you use and the judgements you cast. Practise compassion with regard to how you treat yourself and your ability to cope. Avoid words like 'should', 'must', 'can't', 'problem', 'failure' and 'risk'. Swap them for words such as, 'can', 'could', 'will', 'opportunity' and 'chance'.

5 **Are you going to practise until the strategies become second nature?**

This stuff takes time! You're working at re-educating your brain, teaching it new ways of thinking. As such, you need to practise. Things aren't suddenly going to change. You have to work at it.

6 **Go through the symptom checklist in Chapter 1 again now. Do you notice any changes?**

Are you experiencing any symptoms less frequently or not at all?

7 **Are you going to try to expand your life pie?**

Having more things in your life gives you a fuller life. You can't argue with that. This doesn't mean you neglect what's important – you're just adding more value and meaning to your days. This will protect you from feeling helpless and vulnerable if one thing in your life falters or changes.

8 **Are you going to build up your support network?**

Investigate support groups and maintain the ones you have. Say yes to invitations, invite people to things yourself and don't take your friends or family for granted. Be grateful for them. Consider revealing to them that you're working on your fear and anxiety issues. Their encouragement will make you feel supported and getting another view can be helpful in gaining a new perspective. Also, watch out for mood drains and consider whether they're worth having in your life.

9 **Are you going to take responsibility for your life and accept that you have choices?**

It's not what happens to you that affects you, it's how you *interpret* what happens. No one can force you to think, behave or feel a certain way. You choose. And you can choose to take the better route, to behave bravely, to think positively, to learn from and push through negative emotions.

10 **When are you going to put this new way of being into practice?**

A I already have

B Today

C Next week

D Next month

E Never

There are no right or wrong answers to these questions. It's a personal assessment to see how you're doing and to flag up any areas you'd like to spend more time working on. In today's world we've come to expect everything immediately – information, news and medical 'quick fixes'. There are no quick fixes when it comes to changing ingrained thought and behavioural processes. Habits are built up over years and years so change takes time. Don't let this put you off, though. The harder you work, the sooner you'll see meaningful improvements in how you feel about your own abilities. You should be focused on making changes that last, so you may slip up occasionally, but keep at it. The strategies will work if you continue to use them.

Remember, fear is normal and natural. It's how you deal with it that counts. You choose your path in life. You have power over what happens to you. Choose courage. Choose proactivity. Choose fulfilment. Choose self-belief. Choose all of these things and you'll feel fearless!

Further reading

Robert Leahy, *The Worry Cure* (Piatkus, 2008)

Norman Vincent Peale, *The Power of Positive Thinking* (Random House Group Ltd, 2012 edition)

Helen Kennerly, *Overcoming Anxiety* (Constable & Robinson, 2009)

Gillian Butler, *Overcoming Social Anxiety and Shyness* (Constable & Robinson, 2008)

Useful websites

MIND, The National Association for Mental Health: www.mind.org.uk

Time to Change: www.time-to-change.org.uk

Anxiety UK: www.anxietyuk.org.uk

Moodjuice: www.moodjuice.scot.nhs.uk

Be Mindful: bemindful.co.uk

Mood Gym: moodgym.anu.edu.au

Living Life to the Full: www.llttf.com

The Centre for Clinical Interventions: www.cci.health.wa.gov.au/resources

The Mental Health Foundation: www.mentalhealth.org.uk

The American Mental Health Foundation: americanmentalhealthfoundation.org

The Beck Institute: www.beckinstitute.org

Cruse Bereavement Care: www.cruse.org.uk

Relate: www.relate.org.uk

Frank: friendly confidential drugs advice: www.talktofrank.com

Alcohol Concern: www.alcoholconcern.org.uk

The British Psychological Society: www.bps.org.uk

The British Association for Behavioural & Cognitive Psychotherapy: www.babcp.com

Samaritans: www.samaritans.org

References

P. 81: 'Worry Tree' diagram is an adaptation of the 'Worry Decision Tree' from Butler and Hope, *Managing Your Mind: The Mental Fitness Guide* (Oxford University Press, 2007). Adapted with permission.

P. 84: Sarah Knight, *The Life-Changing Magic of Not Giving a F**k* (London, Quercus, 2015)

P. 102: 'Turn towards your fear' strategy adapted from Christine Dunkley and Maggie Stanton, *Teaching Clients to Use Mindfulness Skills: A Practical Guide* (Routledge, 2013). Adapted with permission.

P. 116: Amy Poehler, *Yes Please* (Picador, 2015)

P. 161: Susan Jeffers, *Feel the Fear and Do It Anyway* (Random House Group Ltd, 2012 edition)

Acknowledgements

First up, a huge THANK YOU to clinical psychologist Dr Richard Irwin for consulting on this book. I couldn't have written this without his expertise, advice and generously given time. Next, to all my family, and especially my husband, Ben, for his encouragement and expert tea-making abilities. To Natasha Hodgson, Jane Sturrock, Charlotte Fry and Alainna Hadjigeorgiou at Quercus for their unfaltering enthusiasm. To my agent Jane Graham Maw for her unwavering support. And to Jo Godfrey Wood and Peggy Sadler at Bookworx for their patience (!) and unsurpassed editing and design skills. Thanks to Beth Hamer for proofreading.

About the author

Jo Usmar is the author of *This Book Will Make You Successful* and the co-author of six other titles in the *This Book Will Make You* series.

Through her work as a journalist for magazines, newspapers and websites including *The Telegraph*, *Huffington Post*, *Stylist*, *ShortList*, *Glamour*, *Cosmopolitan*, the *Mirror* and *Look*, Jo is well known for her entertaining tone and light touch with tricky subjects. She has appeared on Radio 4's *Woman's Hour* and *Sky News* discussing her work and is the founder of the Instagram self-help vlog project *Bite Sized Psych*.

www.jousmar.com

ALSO AVAILABLE

 Successful

 Feel Beautiful

 Sleep

 Calm

 Happy

 Confident

 Mindful

Quercus
www.quercusbooks.co.uk